The War Chief of the Six Nations

Louis Aubrey Wood

Contents

CHAPTER I THE YOUNG MOHAWK 7
CHAPTER II BATTLE OF LAKE GEORGE 11
CHAPTER III SCHOOLDAYS AND AFTER 16
CHAPTER IV THE WAYS DIVIDE 20
CHAPTER V ACROSS THE SEA 25
CHAPTER VI BRANT MEETS HERKIMER 29
CHAPTER VII FORT STANWIX AND ORISKANY 34
CHAPTER VIII FIGHTING ON THE FRONTIER 39
CHAPTER IX CHERRY VALLEY 44
CHAPTER X MINISINK AND THE CHEMUNG RIVER 49
CHAPTER XI OVER THE BORDER 55
CHAPTER XII ENGLAND ONCE MORE 61
CHAPTER XIII STATESMAN OF THE TRIBES 65
CHAPTER XIV THE CHURCH BELL RINGS 71
CHAPTER XV THE PINE-TREE TOTTERS 75

THE WAR CHIEF OF
THE SIX NATIONS

BY
Louis Aubrey Wood

CHAPTER I
THE YOUNG MOHAWK

A group of huntsmen were camping on the Ohio river. The foliage swayed in the night wind, and the argent light of the moon ran in fleeting bars through the dim recesses of the forest. From the ground arose a ruddier glare. High and dry, fires had been built and the flames were darting and curvetting among the trees. In the weird light the hunters were clustered about in squads, silently stripping their prey or preparing their weapons for the morrow's chase. In the background were the women, moving here and there in the dancing shadows. One was bending low over a newborn infant, and as she uttered his name in the stillness of the evening it blended with the music of the tree-tops.

'Thayendanegea!'[1]

The name was taken from the great book of nature. It was a birth-name of the Mohawks meaning two sticks of wood bound together, a sign of strength; and the woman hoped that her tiny child might one day be a man of valour among the Mohawks. Could she have but known it, her desire was to be more than realized, for in vigour of mind and body he was destined to surpass all the offspring of his race.

So it was, in the pear 1742, in the reign of King George the Second, that Thayendanegea was born among the Mohawks on the banks of the Ohio. To the untaught savage this sluggish stream was a thing of life, and he called it the 'River Beautiful.' The Ohio valley was at this time the favourite hunting-ground of the Indian peoples. Because this valley was rich in game and comfortable to dwell in, it had been a scene of bitter strife. The problem of rule on the Ohio was of long standing. For a whole century Delaware and Shawnee and Wyandot and Six Nations contended for the territory; tribe was pitted against tribe, and then at last the

---

1 Pronounced Tai-yen-da-nay-geh.

answer was given. The Iroquois confederacy, or Six Nations,[2] whose villages lay by the Hudson river, united, determined, and vengeful, had gained the ascendancy; from the banks of the Hudson to the seats of the stranger beside lake Erie the lands belonged to them; and other tribes to the east and west and north and south paid them tribute. The Mohawks were the mightiest of the Six Nations; in the confederacy they were chief in council; from their ranks was chosen the head war chief, who commanded on the field of battle; they took the first-fruits of the chase, and were leaders in everything.

Some time was to pass, however, before Thayendanegea could understand that he was sprung from a race of conquerors. As yet he was but a simple Indian babe, with staring brown eyes and raven-black hair. Of the mother who cared for him history has practically nothing to say. She may have been a Mohawk, but this is by no means certain. It has even been hinted that she came from the Western Indians, and was a damsel of the Shawnee race who had left the wigwams of her people. At all events we may be sure that she had the natural instincts and impulses of a forest mother; that she knew where the linden grew high and where the brown-red sycamores clustered thick by the margin of the stream. It may be supposed that when the sun mounted high she would tie the picturesque, richly ornamented baby-frame containing her boy to some drooping branch to swing from its leathern thong in the cooling breeze. We may imagine her tuneful voice singing the mother's Wa Wa song, the soft lullaby of the sylvan glades. Thayendanegea's eyes blink and tremble; he forgets the floating canopy above him and sleeps in his forest cradle.

The hunting excursion to the Ohio came at length to an end, and then the Mohawks started for their lodges in the far north-east. Up the broad river sped the strongest canoe-men of all the peoples of the forest, with Thayendanegea stowed snugly in the bottom of some slender craft. Over the long and weary portages trudged his mother, her child bound loosely on her shoulders. Their route lay towards Lake Erie, then along the well-trodden trail to the Mohawk river; and the baby was for the first time among the fertile cornfields and the strange Long Houses of his people. At this period the Mohawks lived farthest east of all the tribes of the Six Nations. Their main settlements were along the Mohawk river in what is now the state of New York, but they claimed authority over the region stretching thence

---

2   Mohawks, Cayugas, Senecas, Oneidas, Onondagas, and Tuscaroras.

towards Montreal. They had three settlements on the Mohawk, the central one of which, called Canajoharie Castle, was the home of Thayendanegea's parents. Near by lived the celebrated William Johnson, His Majesty's representative for Indian Affairs in the colony of New York, who some years later became sole superintendent of 'the six united nations, their allies and dependents.'

When Thayendanegea grew stronger he began to romp with the other boys of the village. With them he followed the women down to the river's brink, picking up shiny pebbles from the sand, or watching the minnows dart about in the sunlight. With them, when the days were long, he crawled through the brambles, looking for luscious berries, or ran with the wiry Indian dogs into copse and brushwood. Then he learned to swim, to fish, and to dip his paddle noiselessly in the stream. Like every red child, Thayendanegea listened rapt in wonder to the tales that were told him. The Mohawks had a storehouse of fable, and he soon became versed in the lore of the forest. Perhaps, too, he sat beside his wrinkled grandfather, who was a sachem,[3] or petty king, of the Six Nations, and heard the old man tell the romantic story of his trip to England in the pear 1710, when Anne was sovereign queen; heard how five sachems at this time had gone on an embassy for their people and were right royally entertained in the city of London; how, as they passed through the streets, the little children flocked behind, marvelling at their odd appearance; how at the palace they appeared in garments of black and scarlet and gold and were gladly received by the queen, whom they promised to defend against her foes; and how, after seeing the soldiers march, and after riding in the queen's barge and enjoying various amusements, they returned to their own country.

There is some obscurity surrounding the identity of Thayendanegea's father, but it is generally agreed that he was a full-blooded Mohawk and a chief of the Wolf clan.[4] By some writers it is said that he bore the English name of Nickus Brant. Others say that Thayendanegea's father died while the son was still an infant and that the mother then married an Indian known to the English as Brant. By and by, as Thayendanegea mingled with the English, he acquired the name of Joseph, and

---

3 That Thayendanegea was the grandchild of one of these sachems who were so honoured appears from information given in an article published in the London Magazine; of July 1776. The material for this account of him is supposed to have been supplied by the famous author James Boswell, with whom, while on a visit to England in that year, he was intimate.

4 The Mohawks were divided into three clans--the Tortoise, the Bear, and the Wolf.

so came down through history as Joseph Brant; but whether he acquired this name from his father or from his step-father we cannot tell, and it does not really matter. We shall know him hereafter by his English name.

In the traditions of the Mohawk valley it is told how one day a regimental muster was being held, in Tryon county, in the colony of New York, at which William Johnson was present. Among the throng of those who were out to see the sights was Molly Brant, Joseph's elder sister, a lively, winsome girl of sixteen years. During the manoeuvres a field-officer rode by, mounted on a spirited steed. As he passed, Molly asked if she might get up behind. The officer, thinking it a bit of banter, said she might. In an instant she had sprung upon the crupper. Away went the steed, flying about the field. Molly clung tight to the officer, her blanket flapping in the breeze and her dark hair floating wide. Every one burst into merriment, and no one enjoyed the spectacle more than Colonel William Johnson himself. A flame of love for Molly was kindled in his heart, and, being a widower, he took her home and made her his bride after the Indian fashion. It would seem quite natural, then, that the superintendent should be interested in the career of Molly's brother Joseph. Born, as the young redskin was, of princely stock, he might, with such an advantage, be expected to attain to honour and dignity among the people of the Long House. There was, however, one obstacle; although Joseph's father was a chief, he did not inherit rank, for it was the custom of the Six Nations to trace descent through the blood of the mother, and his mother, who had brought him over hill and water from the banks of the Ohio, was of humble origin. If Joseph wished, therefore, to rise among his fellows, he must hew out his own path to greatness. By pluck and wisdom alone could he win a lasting place in the hearts of his people. As we tell his story, we shall see how he gathered strength and became a man of might and of valour.

CHAPTER II
BATTLE OF LAKE GEORGE

No one delighted more in the free and easy life of the frontier than did Colonel William Johnson. He was a typical colonial patroon, a representative of the king and a friend of the red man. The Indians trusted him implicitly. He had studied their character and knew well their language. He entered into their life with full sympathy for their traditions and was said to possess an influence over them such as had never been gained by any other white man. For a long time he lived at Fort Johnson, a three-storey dwelling of stone on the left bank of the Mohawk, and later at Johnson Hall, a more spacious mansion several miles farther north. Here all who came were treated with a lavish hand, and the wayfarer found a welcome as he stopped to admire the flowers which grew before the portals. Within were a retinue of servants, careful for the needs of all. When hearts were sad or time went slowly, a dwarf belonging to the household played a merry tune on his violin to drive away gloom from the wilderness mansion.

On one occasion, however, Johnson's hospitality was taxed beyond all bounds. This was at Fort Johnson in the year 1755, just after he had been made a major-general in the colonial militia. The French from Canada had already been making bold encroachments on territory claimed by the English to the north and the west. They had erected Fort Duquesne at the junction of the Alleghany and Monongahela rivers, where the great city of Pittsburgh now stands; they had fortified Niagara; and now they were bidding defiance to all the English colonists between the Alleghany Mountains and the sea. War had not been declared in Europe, but the inhabitants of the Thirteen Colonies, only too eager to stay the hand of France in America, planned a series of blows against the enemy. Among other things, they decided that an attempt should be made to capture the French stronghold of Fort

Frederic at Crown Point on Lake Champlain. The officer selected to Command the expedition to be sent on this enterprise was William Johnson, now a major-general of the colony of New York.

It flashed at once across Johnson's mind that his redskin friends could aid him in the undertaking; so he sent messages with all speed to the tribes, asking them to gather at his house. Eleven hundred hungry Indians answered the summons. From all quarters they came in, taking up their residence for the time being upon his broad domain. Johnson's bright and genial face clouded as he looked upon the multitude of guests and saw his food supplies vanishing and every green thing that grew upon his fields and meadows being plucked up. But he bore it all good-naturedly, for he was determined to win their support. Seated on the grass in squads, according to their tribes, they listened while he addressed them and told them of their duties to the English crown. With rising eloquence he said that they were bound in their allegiance to the English as though with a silver chain. 'The ends of this silver chain,' he added, 'are fixed in the immovable mountains, in so firm a manner that the hands of no mortal enemy might be able to move it.' Then as he bade them take the field, he held a war belt in his hands and exclaimed with fervour:

'My war kettle is on the fire; my canoe is ready to put into the water; my gun is loaded; my sword is by my side; and my axe is sharpened.'

Little Abraham, sachem of the lower Mohawk valley, took the belt from him, Red Head, a chief of the Onondagas, made reply, telling him that from every castle warriors would follow him to the north. A war dance followed, and a large body of the Six Nations were ready for the fray.

No doubt young Joseph Brant was in this great audience, listening to the speeches of his elders. He was only thirteen years of age at the time, but the spirit of the war-path was already upon him. The zealous appeals of the major-general must have stirred him greatly, and it may well be that this lad, with youthful frame and boyish features, here received an impulse which often sustained him in later years during his long career of active loyalty on behalf of the English cause. As it happened, Joseph was soon to be in active service. On August 8, 1755, Johnson's expedition left Albany, and a week later arrived at the great carrying-place between the Hudson and Lac St Sacrement, as Lake George was then called. At this point Fort

Lyman[5] had been built the same summer. Thence the major-general set out, with fifteen hundred provincials and three hundred Indians, on his journey northward. King Hendrick, a chief of the Mohawks, led the tribesmen, and under his direction a number of braves were being tested for the first time. One of these--we may imagine the boy's intense delight--was young Joseph Brant.

On reaching Lac St Sacrement Johnson made a halt and took up a strong position on the shore. Soon reinforcements arrived under General Phineas Lyman, his second in command. Johnson re-named the lake. 'I have given it,' he says, 'the name of Lake George, not only in honour of His Majesty, but to assert his undoubted dominion here.'

Meanwhile Baron Dieskau, the commander of the French forces, having landed at South Bay, the southern extremity of the waters of Lake Champlain, was moving down through the woods. His army was made up of a large body of French Canadians, Indians, and regular soldiers of the regiments of La Reine and Languedoc. He marched by way of Wood Creek, and was bent on making a vigorous attack on Fort Lyman. But when he arrived at a point about midway between Fort Lyman and Johnson's camp on Lake George, his Indians became unruly, declaring that they would march no farther south nor venture off the soil that belonged to France. There was nothing for Dieskau to do but to change his plans. Swerving in a north-westerly direction, he struck the new road that Johnson had made to the lake. This he followed, intending to fall upon the English forces wherever he should find them.

Johnson's scouts, prowling to the southward, detected this move. Back to the encampment they brought the news of Dieskau's approach and the English leader at once made ready to defend his position. Trees were felled; the wagons and bateaux were brought up; a strong breastwork was built across the new-cut roadway; cannon were put in position to play upon the advancing enemy. Then discussion took place as to the advisability of making a sortie against the foe. It was suggested that five hundred men would be sufficient, but at the mention of this number King Hendrick, the Indian leader, interposed. What, indeed, could such a paltry handful do in the face of the oncoming Frenchmen?

'If they are to fight,' he said, 'they are too few; if they are to be killed, they are

---

5   Afterwards named Fort Edward.

too many.'

In the early morning, September 8, 1755, a force of twelve hundred set forth, only to learn the wisdom of Hendrick's advice. Dieskau was proceeding cautiously, hoping to catch the English in a trap. He sent out flying wings of Indians and Canadians, while his French regulars formed the centre of his force. As the English advanced along the road, they found themselves suddenly attacked on both sides by the enemy. A stiff struggle then took place in which Johnson's men were badly worsted. King Hendrick's horse was shot down, and before he could free himself from his saddle he was slain by a bayonet thrust. Retreat now became necessary, and by a steady movement the English fell back upon their camp. There they determined to make a decisive stand. Dieskau, emboldened by the success of his previous advance, led his troops towards the lake in battle array. His progress, however, was stopped by the rude barricade which had been piled across the road, and by eleven o'clock the second engagement of the day was already being fought.

Brant has described his feelings when, as a mere boy, he received his baptism of fire upon this battle-ground. When the clatter of the musketry fell upon his ears, his heart jumped and an indescribable fear seemed to take possession of him. His limbs trembled, and in despair he looked for something to steady him in the ordeal. Near by grew a slender sapling, and he clutched at this and held on tenaciously while the bullets went whizzing by. After a few volleys had been fired he regained his natural poise and took his place beside the old fighters who were holding their own against a savage attack. From this moment he acquitted himself with valour in the battle, and, youth though he was, he fulfilled his desire 'to support the character of a brave man of which he was exceedingly ambitious.'

At length the French troops began to recoil before the sweep of the English cannon. Dieskau received a severe wound and the ardour of his followers was visibly cooled. At four o'clock the English general thought the opportune moment had arrived to make a sortie, and his men climbed over the rampart and drove the French to flight in every direction. The wounded Dieskau was made prisoner and borne to the camp of his enemy. Johnson's leg had been pierced by a bullet, and in this condition he was carried to his tent.

As the two generals lay helpless on their litters, several redskins entered the tent and scowled upon the recumbent Dieskau. 'These fellows have been regarding me with a look not indicative of much compassion,' said the French commander. 'Anything else!' answered Johnson, 'for they wished to oblige me to deliver you into their hands in order to burn you, in revenge for the death of their comrades and of their chiefs who have been slain in the battle.' Then he added: 'Feel no uneasiness; you are safe with me.'

This affair at Lake George was only an opening battle in the Seven Years' War between France and England which was waged in three continents and closed in America with the fall of Montreal in 1760. For his victory over Dieskau William Johnson was made a baronet, and thus became Sir William Johnson. He continued to offer his services until the war ended; and during the memorable campaign of 1759, while Wolfe and Amherst were operating in the east, he was sent with Brigadier Prideaux to effect, if possible, the capture of Fort Niagara. The expedition ascended the Mohawk in June, crossed over to Oswego, and thence followed the south shore of Lake Ontario to its destination. The French fort stood at the mouth of the Niagara where it enters Lake Ontario, and was under the command of Captain Pouchot. No sooner had this officer heard of the English approach than he sent to Presqu'Ile and other points in the west asking that reinforcements should be dispatched with all haste for his relief.

The English investing army consisted of twenty-three hundred regulars and provincials, together with nine hundred Indians from the tribes of the Six Nations. At the very outset Prideaux was accidentally killed by the premature bursting of a shell from a coehorn and Johnson had to take command. Acting with vigour he prosecuted the siege until July 24, when firing in the distance told that help for the besieged would soon be at hand. Straightway Johnson selected one-third of his men and marched to meet the relieving force, which was led by Captain D'Aubrey and comprised eleven hundred French and several hundred redskins from the western tribes. The conflict which ensued was short but desperate. The Six Nations, posted on the flanks of the English line, fought valiantly, and, largely owing to their valour, the French were put to rout. On the same day Pouchot capitulated. By this success the chain of French forts stretching from the St Lawrence to Louisiana was snapped near the middle. Although Brant's deeds have not been recorded, it is stated on good authority that he was with Sir William Johnson on this occasion and that he bore himself with marked distinction.

CHAPTER III
SCHOOLDAYS AND AFTER

Through the storm and stress of these campaigns, the eyes of the Mohawks were upon Joseph Brant. They expected much of him, and he earnestly tried to fulfil their hopes. Still in his teens, he was already a seasoned warrior, having 'fought with Death and dulled his sword.' The Mohawks were pleased. Let a few more autumns strew the carpet of the forest, and they would have in him a brave and robust leader worthy of their tradition. Joseph, on the other hand, was dissatisfied. He had lived and communed with white men and had come to know a greatness that was not to be won by following the war-path. He had wielded the tomahawk; he had bivouacked among armed men on the field of battle: now he was eager for the schoolroom. He wished to widen his knowledge and to see the great world that lay beyond the rude haunts of the red men.

Joseph was in this frame of mind when an Indian with the very English name of David Fowler came to Fort Johnson. Fowler was on a long journey from his home by the sea and rode on horseback. He had something to relate, he said, that was of significance for the Indian people. At Lebanon, in the colony of Connecticut, there was an institution for the education of any young redskin who might be able to come, and he had been sent by Doctor Eleazar Wheelock, its principal, to gather recruits. Addressing Sir William Johnson, he asked him if there were among the Six Nations Indians any lads whom he should like to send to the school.

Sir William was not slow to act. Joseph Brant, the pride of Canajoharie Castle, thirsting for knowledge, must surely go. Two other boys, named Negyes and Center, were chosen to accompany him. These were 'three boys,' as Dr Wheelock afterwards wrote, 'who were willing to leave their friends and country, and come among strangers of another language and quite another manner of living, and where, perhaps, none of their nation, then living, had ever been.'

The trip to Connecticut was made in 1761, and the lads arrived at Lebanon about mid-summer. They were not at all sure that the school would be to their liking and had planned, if such should prove to be the case, to make a hasty flight back to the Mohawk valley on the horses they brought with them. Negyes and Center looked rather woebegone as they came into Dr Wheelock's presence: 'Two of them,' he says, 'were but little better than naked.' Brant, however, created a good impression. 'The other, being of a family of distinction, was considerably clothed, Indian fashion, and could speak a few words of English.'

The school was kept up by a number of benevolent persons who contributed liberally to its funds. Sir William Johnson was ready to do his share to aid the good work, and some four months and a half after the Mohawk boys had arrived he wrote to the principal: 'I shall not be backward to contribute my mite.' A house in which to hold the classes and two acres of land had been given by a farmer named Joshua Moor; hence the institution was generally called Moor's Indian Charity School. The principal, Dr Wheelock, was a man of wide scholarship, and became later on the founder of the seat of learning in New Hampshire now known as Dartmouth College.

But little is known of the course of study pursued by Joseph at Moor's School. When he entered it his knowledge must have been very slender, and as a young man he began to learn things ordinarily taught to a mere child. It is likely that he now became much more fluent than formerly in his use of the English tongue. From the beginning his progress was very rapid, and Dr Wheelock does not stint the praise that he bestows upon him: 'Joseph is indeed an excellent youth,' was his comment; 'he has much endeared himself to me, as well as to his master, and everybody also by his good behaviour.'

The master here spoken of was Charles Jeffrey Smith, a young man of ample means who wished to be of service to the Indians. He had come to the school after Joseph's arrival and helped the principal in giving instruction. He very soon remarked the superior intelligence which Joseph showed among the twenty-five pupils in his charge. Intending to make a missionary tour among the Indian tribes, he proposed to take his young pupil with him as an interpreter. Writing to Sir William Johnson about the matter, he referred to Joseph in most glowing terms: 'As he is a promising youth, of a sprightly genius, singular modesty, and a serious turn, I know of none so well calculated to answer my end as he is.'

It was with sad misgivings that Joseph thought of turning his back upon the school, where he had been for scarcely two years; but Smith promised to continue as his teacher when they were together in the Indian country, and to pay him something for his work as an interpreter. This appealed to the young redskin. It appeared that his schooldays were ended in any event, for his people were jealous of his prolonged stay in the lodges of the stranger and he had received a message calling him back to Canajoharie Castle.

In the month of June 1763, master and pupil set out together, but, as fate would have it, Smith's quest among the tribes was to be quickly ended. Hardly had he begun his pilgrimage when he found the Indians in wild commotion. Again the hatchet had been unburied, and for the sake of security he had to bring his mission to an abrupt end.

Pontiac, great chief of the Ottawas, had raised the standard of revolt against English rule. This was an aftermath of the struggle just concluded with France, and began when the Western Indians saw that another race of pale-faces had come upon their lands. With skill and adroitness Pontiac had gathered many tribes into a strong offensive league. He declared that if they followed in his train he would drive the feet of the intruder from the red man's territory. There was a savage rising in May 1763. In a twinkling eight English posts in the interior fell before the savages. Fort Ligonier and Fort Pitt,[6] at the head-waters of the Ohio, and Fort Detroit in the west, were alone left standing of all the places attacked, and Detroit was besieged by Pontiac with thirty-six chiefs at his back. The call to arms in defence was urgent. A portion of the Six Nations joined their old allies, the English, and among the warriors who went out was Joseph Brant. 'Joseph tarried,' we are told, 'and went out with a company against the Indians, and was useful in the war, in which he behaved so much like the Christian and the soldier, that he gained great esteem.'

A body of Mohawks were among the troops which brought succour to Major Gladwyn in his resistance at Fort Detroit in 1763, and it is possible that Brant was in the thick of the fight in this vicinity. It is possible, too, that he was with Colonel Bouquet in August at the battle of Bushy Run, near Fort Pitt. In this engagement,

---

6 Formerly Fort Duquesne.

after two days of strenuous backwoods fighting, the Indians were finally worsted. Pontiac's star had begun to set. With hopeless odds against him, the stubborn chief of the Ottawas kept up the struggle until the following year, but at last he was compelled to sue for peace.

In the meantime Brant's reputation among his tribesmen was steadily rising. In the spring of 1764, when the fighting was at an end, he returned to Canajoharie Castle. There he built a comfortable house, wedded the daughter of an Oneida chieftain, and dwelt for some years in peace and quiet. Two children, Isaac and Christiana, were born to him of this, his first, marriage. We may pass rapidly over these tranquil years of Brant's life. He did his domestic duties as a man should; and Sir William Johnson, finding him trustworthy, had constant work for him, and sent him on many important missions to the Indians, even to the far-western tribes. During this period Brant became a communicant in the Anglican Church, and, knowing well what hardships the missionaries had to endure, he gave them what help he could in their work among the red people. He assisted the Rev. John Stuart, a missionary to his tribe and afterwards a distinguished clergyman in Upper Canada, in his translation of the Acts of the Apostles, in a History of the Bible, and in a brief explanation of the Catechism, in the dialect of the Mohawks. It is related that a belated missionary, footsore and weary, crept one day to Brant's abode, where he was given food and cared for in his sickness. 'Joseph Brant,' the missionary wrote in grateful tribute, 'is exceeding kind.'

It was well that a man of judicious mind and fearless heart was coming to the fore among the nation of the Mohawks. A cloud had begun to fleck the horizon; soon would come the sound of the approaching tempest. How would it fare with the Six Nations in the day of turmoil?

CHAPTER IV
THE WAYS DIVIDE

The happy ending, in 1763, of the war with France left the English colonies in America with little to disturb them, except the discontented red men beyond the Alleghany Mountains. The colonies grew larger; they did more business and they gathered more wealth. But as they prospered they became self-confident and with scarce an enemy at home they became involved in a quarrel with the motherland across the sea. England, they said, was taxing them unjustly and posting soldiers in their chief cities to carry out her will. They were by no means disposed to submit. As early as 1770 a mob in Boston attacked an English guard and drew upon themselves its fire, which caused bloodshed in the city's streets. This was the prelude of the American Revolution. A brief lull came in the storm. But as Britain still insisted on the right to tax the colonies and made an impost on tea the test of her right, rebels in Boston accepted the challenge and were inflamed to violence; they swarmed on a tea-ship which had entered the bay, dragged the packets from the hold, and cast them into the waters of the harbour. When news of this act of violence reached England, parliament passed a bill providing for the shutting up of the port of Boston and removing the seat of government to Salem. In 1774 General Gage, the recently appointed governor of Massachusetts, placed the colony under military rule, and it was cut off from the rest of the country. The signal for revolt was thus given, and a general revolution soon followed.

The colonists immediately divided into two parties; on the one side were those who felt that they must obey what they thought to be the call of liberty; on the other were those who had no desire, and felt no need, to follow a summons to insurrection against His Majesty the King. The red man began to see clearly that the whites, the 'Long Knives,' brethren of the same race, would soon be at one another's throats, and that they, the natives, could not remain neutral when the war broke out.

During these alarming days Sir William Johnson died, when scarcely sixty years of age. He had seen that the break with the motherland was coming, and the prospect was almost more than he could bear. On the very day of his death he had received dispatches from England that probably hastened his end. He was told, under the royal seal, of the great peril that lay in store for all the king's people, and he was urged to keep the Six Nations firm in their allegiance to the crown. On that morning, July 11, 1774, the dying man called the Indians to council, and spoke what were to be his parting words to the tribes. They must, he said, stand by the king, undaunted and unmoved under every trial. A few hours later the gallant Sir William Johnson, the friend of all the sons of the forest, the guide and helper of Joseph Brant, had breathed his last. His estates and titles were inherited by his son John Johnson, who was also promoted to the rank of major-general in the army. The control of Indian Affairs passed into the hands of his son-in-law, Colonel Guy Johnson, an able man, but less popular and wanting the broad sympathies of the great superintendent. Brant was at once made secretary to Guy Johnson, and to these two men Sir William's work of dealing with the Indians now fell. Their task, laid on them by their king, was to keep the Six Nations true to his cause in the hour when the tomahawk should leave its girdle and the war fires should again gleam sullenly in the depths of the forest.

Joseph Brant set about this work with restless energy. He was no longer the stripling who had gone away to the West that he might aid in bending the pride of Pontiac. Ten years had passed, and now he was a mature man with an ever-broadening vision. Some time during these years he had reached the position among his tribesmen which he long had coveted. He had been recognized by the Mohawks as one of their chieftains. This honour he had won by right not of birth but of merit, and for this reason he was known as a 'Pine-tree Chief.' Like the pine-tree, tall and strong and conspicuous among the trees of the forest, he had achieved a commanding place in the Mohawk nation. True, he was a chief merely by gift of his tribe, but he seems, nevertheless, to have been treated with the same respect and confidence as the hereditary chiefs. He rejoiced in his new distinction. Evil days were ahead, and he was now in a position to do effective work on behalf of his people and of the

British when the inevitable war should break out. A still greater honour was in store for him. When war was declared he at once became recognized as the war leader of the Six Nations--the War Chief. The hereditary successor of King Hendrick, who was slain at Lake George in 1755, was Little Abraham; but Little Abraham, it appears, desired to remain neutral in the impending struggle, and by common consent Brant assumed the leadership of the Iroquois in war.

Two things favoured Brant in any appeal he might make in the interests of the British to the loyalty of the Six Nations. For over a hundred years they had taken from the colonial agents who represented the crown wampum belts as a sign of treaty obligations. Treaties had been made with the king; the word of the red man had been given to the king. Promises made to them by the king's agents had always been performed. Why, therefore, should they now plight their faith to any other than their Great Father the King, who dwelt far over the waters? Besides, by recent actions of the colonists, the resentment of the Indians had been fanned to a fury. In 1774 some colonial land-hunters were scouring the country of the Shawnees. Without any real cause they fell upon some redskins and butchered several in an inhuman way. Not satisfied with this act of cruelty, they seized two brave chiefs, Bald Eagle and Silver Heels, and killed them in cold blood. The anger of the Indians was aroused and they rallied under the banner of the noble Logan, 'Mingo Chief' of the Shawnees. Against him the Virginians sent a large force of more than two thousand men. A fierce battle took place at the Great Kanawha river, at the point where that stream flows into the Ohio. For a time Logan and his Indian ally Cornstalk and their followers fought desperately, but in the end they were forced to flee across the Ohio. This war was short, indeed, but it had no just warrant, and the Indians could not forget the outrage that had been committed. The memory of it rankled with the Six Nations, especially among the Cayugas, to whom Logan was bound by ties of blood.

While Joseph was doing his utmost to keep the Indians loyal and was keeping watch upon those who were plotting to win them from their allegiance to the crown, Sir John Johnson was growing anxious for his own life. So great was his, fear of being killed or abducted that he increased his body-guard to five hundred men. At the same time, he placed swivel-guns about his house, in order to withstand a sudden attack. He energetically organized the settlers on his domains into a protecting force. In particular the Highland loyalists in his district rallied to his aid, and soon a hundred and fifty brawny clansmen were ready to take the field at the shortest notice.

But the Six Nations were by no means united in their loyalty to the crown. Brant saw that the tribe most wavering in its support was the Oneidas. He found that their missionary, Samuel Kirkland, was in league with the rebels, and sought to have this clergyman removed. Failing in this, he wrote to the Oneida chiefs, urging them to remain loyal to the king. A letter that an Oneida runner let fall at this time on an Indian path is the earliest bit of handwriting that we have from Joseph Brant's pen. In it he warns the Oneidas against the subtle work which the colonists were carrying on. 'Guy Johnson is in great fear of being taken prisoner by the Bostonians,' he says. 'We Mohawks are obliged to watch him constantly. Guy Johnson assures himself, and depends upon your coming to his assistance... He believes not that you will assent to let him suffer.' The appeal thus made seems, however, to have met with little response from the Oneidas, and Brant was rebuffed. Even before this they had sent a letter to the governor of Connecticut expressing in, plain terms their desire to remain neutral when hostilities should commence. 'We cannot intermeddle in this dispute between two brothers,' was their decision. 'The quarrel seems to be unnatural.' The Oneidas had the right to their opinion, but their conduct must have stung the heart of the chief of the Mohawks. Yet never for a moment did his courage fail. He knew that the bulk of the Six Nations were willing to give their life's blood in the service of the king. He and they would be true to the old and binding covenant which their forefathers had made as allies of the crown. 'It will not do for us to break it,' said Brant, 'let what will become of us.'

Civil war was now impending in the colonies. The battle of Lexington had been fought, and the whole country was taking breath before the plunge into the conflict. Guy Johnson and Brant were waiting to declare themselves and the time was nearly ripe. The first move was made just after the Mohawk chiefs had been summoned to a council at Guy Park,[7] about the end of May. Secret orders had come from General Gage, and Johnson knew precisely what course he was expected to follow. Leaving his house to what fate might befall it, he started westward with

---

7 'A beautiful situation immediately on the bank of the Mohawk. The elegant stone mansion is yet [1865] upon the premises giving the best evidence of substantial building.'--William L. Stone, *Life of Joseph Brant*, vol. i. p. 71.

Brant and a force of Indians and white men. At their first important stopping-place, Cosby's Manor, a letter was sent back to throw a blind across their trail. Then, with their faces still towards the setting sun, the loyal band wended their way through the dark mazes of the forest.

After a weary journey the loyalist party emerged among the populous western villages of the Iroquois confederacy. There, at Ontario, south of the lake of that name, was held a great assembly, and fifteen hundred warriors listened to the messengers of the king. In reply the chiefs of the assembled throng expressed their willingness to 'assist his Majesty's troops in their operations.' Johnson and Brant then went on to Oswego, on the margin of the lake, where an even larger body heard their plea. Johnson prepared for the redskins a typical repast, and 'invited them to feast on a Bostonian.' The Indians avowed their willingness to fight for the king. Then, while the summer days were long, a flotilla of canoes, in which were many of the most renowned chiefs of the Six Nations, set out eastward for Montreal over the sparkling waters of Lake Ontario. In one of the slender craft knelt Joseph Brant, paddle in hand, thoughtful and yet rejoicing. He was but thirty-three years old, and yet, by shrewdness in council and by courage on the field of battle, he already occupied a prominent place among the chiefs of the confederacy. Moreover, great days were ahead. Soon the canoes entered the broad St Lawrence and were gliding swiftly among its islets. With steady motion they followed its majestic course as it moved towards the sea.

CHAPTER V
ACROSS THE SEA

Before many suns had set, this company of dusky warriors had brought their canoes to shore near the swift rapids which run by Montreal. The news of their coming was received with enthusiasm by the officers stationed at this place. Every friendly addition to the British ranks was of value now that war had begun. Sir Guy Carleton, the governor of Canada, was especially delighted that these bronzed stalwarts had made their appearance. He prized the abilities of the Indians in border warfare, and their arrival now might be of importance, since the local Canadian militia had not responded to the call to arms. The French seigneurs and clergy were favourable to the king's cause, but the habitants on the whole were not interested in the war, and Carleton's regular troops consisted of only eight hundred men of the Seventh and Twenty-Sixth regiments.

No time was lost by the governor in summoning the redskins to an interview. Chief Brant, it appears, was the leading spokesman for the Indians on this occasion, and a sentence or two of the speech made by Carleton has been preserved by Brant himself. 'I exhort you,' was Carleton's earnest request of the Indians, 'to continue your adherence to the King, and not to break the solemn agreement made by your forefathers, for your own welfare is intimately connected with your continuing the allies of his Majesty.' In reply the Indians asserted once more their ancient pledges. 'We acknowledged,' said Brant, 'that it would certainly be the best in the end for our families and ourselves to remain under the King's protection, whatever difficulties we might have to contend with.'

In order that he might render due service to the army, Brant was put under military discipline, and was given a captain's commission in the king's forces. He was in Montreal when Ethan Allen, a colonial adventurer, made an unauthorized attempt (Sept. 24, 1775) to surprise and capture the city. Carleton had been apprised of Allen's project; the plan miscarried, and Allen, along with other members of his band, was sent to England as a prisoner of war. Meanwhile General Montgomery had been advancing from the south, and, in September, he laid siege to Fort St John, the English stronghold on the Richelieu river. This post was stoutly defended by Major Preston with a force of regulars until Fort Chambly, near by, fell into the enemy's hands, and further resistance was useless. Whether Brant's services were employed in or about either of these forts cannot be ascertained, but we know that he had left the neighbourhood and was on his way to England before Montreal capitulated on November 17.

Brant's visit to Montreal had no doubt an important influence on his career. This was perhaps the first time he had ever seen a sea-port.[8] At this time Montreal had some five or six thousand inhabitants and was a walled town of growing commercial importance. It had several commodious religious houses, some large, well-built churches, and a number of handsome residences. As Brant stood on the river's bank, he saw a medley of craft afloat in the current: ships of the fur traders laden with peltry; transports coming and going with food for the garrisons, or new men for the service; sloops-of-war, lying at anchor with their complement of guns, grim and menacing.

All this gripped as with an iron hand the imaginative nature of the Mohawk chief. The spirit of romance was aglow within him, and he had a wondering desire to see the lands that lay beyond the ocean. He would sail upon the high seas; he would stand in the presence of the Great King. How beautiful was this land called England! and how powerful were its army and navy! Doubtless Guy Johnson and other officers at Montreal encouraged Brant to undertake the journey which he fain would make. It may be that it was they who first showed him how such a journey was possible. At any rate, before the ice had begun to lock the green waters of the St Lawrence, in the year 1775, he had passed through the Gulf and was tossing on the billows of the deep Atlantic. Towards the end of the year he arrived, along with Captain Tice, in the English metropolis. London had altered greatly since the days of Queen Anne more than half a century before, when his grandfather had been there. It had become a greater market for trade, and the common people had been

---

8 It is thought possible that he had gone down the St Lawrence as far as Montreal with Sir William Johnson in 1760.

elbowing their way to the parts where only fine residences had once stood. Two kings of the House of Hanover had in the meantime reigned and died, and now King George III, another of that line, sat upon the throne.

On reaching London Chief Brant was escorted to a small hostel of not very imposing appearance called 'The Swan with Two Necks.' It was intended that he should soon be taken to other lodgings that would be more in keeping with his rank; but the innkeeper and others were so kind to him that he was loth to leave, and could not be coaxed to other quarters during his whole stay in London. In the streets he was accustomed to dress like the Europeans of the day, but on state occasions he wore a gala costume, his head crowned with waving plumes and his body decked with those fancy ornaments that pleased the proud Indian. On the burnished tomahawk that glistened in his belt was traced the initial 'J,' followed by his Indian title, 'Thayendanegea.'

Brant appeared at court and had audience with the king, for whose person he felt a sacred reverence. He loved freedom, but at the same time he always had a great respect for authority. A story is told of the pointed answer he made to his old instructor, Dr Wheelock, who, thinking to draw Brant over to the side of the colonists, or at least to keep him neutral, had written him a long and earnest appeal. The Mohawk chief replied in a kindly fashion, referring to the pleasant hours he had spent at the school. He remembered especially the prayers that were said in the household, and one prayer in particular that had been repeated over and over again; as they bent their heads in entreaty before the Maker of all things, the request had ever been 'that they might be able to live as good subjects, to fear God and honour the King.'

Not only did high officials in London treat Brant with consideration, but men of learning, as well as of social position, vied with one another to make his visit interesting and pleasant. Among those who entertained him was James Boswell, who knew all the gossip of London society and was a man of rare talents. He took a peculiar liking to the bronzed chief of the Six Nations and persuaded him to sit for his portrait. The Earl of Warwick also wished to have Brant's picture, and the result was that he sat for George Romney, one of the most famous artists of the day. This portrait was probably painted at the artist's house in Cavendish Square, and we may accept it as a good likeness of Brant as he appeared at this time. With head erect, the strong-knit figure of the chief stands at repose. The eyes are mild and wide-set and about the lips a smile is playing. In the portrait we see, too, the resolute heart, the thoughtful mind, and the restless energy that made Joseph Brant a ruler of the native races.

On being asked as to the help he might render to the English arms in the New World, Brant asserted strongly that he and his people were loyal. He said that, as War Chief, he would lead three thousand of his warriors into the struggle, and that they would fight manfully as subjects of the king. He knew full well how desperate the contest was going to be, and wishing to have some article on his body that would identify him in case of death, he bought from a London goldsmith a ring, in which he had his full name engraved. This he wore through the vicissitudes of many a long year.

Before the winter was over Brant was anxious to return to his tribes, for he knew that when the hatchet was whirling the wigwam was more fitting for him that the palaces of London. Accordingly, in the spring of 1776, he set out for his western home.

CHAPTER VI
BRANT MEETS HERKIMER

When the ship on which Brant was a passenger touched the shores of America, he was landed secretly somewhere near New York city. He was now face to face with the difficulty of reaching his friends--a task that called forth all his alertness. He was in a hostile country, a long way from the forests of the Mohawk valley lying above Albany. But he was a wily redskin, too clever to be caught, and after adroitly evading many dangers he eventually reached the border country and crossed over safely into Canada.

In July 1776, several weeks before his arrival, the colonists had declared their independence. The language of the Declaration of Independence was confident, but soon after it was uttered the colonists suffered a series of defeats. Arnold was beaten by Carleton on Lake Champlain and Washington was forced to retreat until he had crossed the Delaware. It has been said that Brant took part in the Battle of the Cedars, where, on the north bank of the St Lawrence, Captain Forster overpowered a body of four hundred Americans; but this occurred in May 1776, and since Brant's ship did not arrive until July he could not have been one of the combatants in this engagement. What Brant was doing during the greater part of the year following his arrival in Canada has not been recorded. In the spring of 1777 we are able to pick up his trail again. While the armies were preparing for another summer campaign, Brant returned once more to his old haunts near the frontier of the colony of New York, taking up his position at a place called Oquaga on the Susquehanna river, south of the Mohawk valley. This was a favourite resort of the Indians, and Brant was well aware that from this point he could carry on to advantage a guerrilla warfare against the rebels and their sympathizers.

His coming sent a shiver of dread through all the neighbouring settlements.

Hitherto this part of the colony had been remote from the main theatre of the war, but now that Brant was there any moment might bring an attack, and the inhabitants began to make ready their defences. More particularly were steps for protection taken in Cherry Valley, a rich and fertile area stretching up towards the Mohawk. Because of its strength and situation, the house of Colonel Samuel Campbell, one of the prominent farmers in the valley, was selected for a fortified post, and logs and earth were banked about it and the two adjoining barns. Thither from all sides the people collected, thinking that at any moment the chief of the Mohawks might pounce upon them.

Brant did, indeed, intend to assail this fortress, as it contained many of the leading rebels of that district, but a strange incident deceived him with regard to the strength of the place and made him change his purpose. It was not a common thing for him to make errors of judgement, but for once he was misled--hoodwinked--in a very simple manner. Like a wise commander he had set out to reconnoitre the enemy's position, and proceeded in the direction of Campbell's house with a small body of men. When about a mile away, he concealed himself behind some thick shrubbery on the crest of a hillock. As he peered through the tangled foliage his view was obscured, and he descried what seemed to him to be a battalion of troops marching near the house. This was nothing more than a number of boys with wooden guns in their hands playing at soldiers and parading in great glee upon the grassy sward beside the fortified house; but so well did they perform that Brant imagined they were soldiers training for active service in the war. 'Colonel Campbell has got his house well guarded, I perceive,' he said, turning about and addressing his followers. Thinking that it would be folly to venture near the spot with his slender force, Brant decided to retire and he took the road leading towards the Mohawk river. The same evening, as he lay in wait with his men behind a large boulder, two horsemen approached. One was an officer named Wormwood, the other a settler. Without having suspected an ambush, they suddenly found themselves in the clutches of an enemy. In the struggle Lieutenant Wormwood met his death, much to Brant's sorrow, as they had been good friends before the war. After this event the chief returned to Oquaga.

As the weeks passed, his following on the Susquehanna grew apace. The name of the great War Chief had a charm about it that drew to his command warriors from every part of the forest. Little wonder that the settlers became more and more alarmed. At length they resolved to try to negotiate peace with him. One of their number, Nicholas Herkimer, decided to go to the Susquehanna and there have an interview with the chief himself. Herkimer was a citizen noted for his integrity and had been made a brigadier-general in the provincial army. He had formerly lived three miles from Brant, when his home was on the upper Mohawk, and knew him well. Nothing has ever been said to show that Herkimer lacked courage. But he was vain enough to think that a few words from him might weaken Brant's steadfast loyalty. Furthermore, like too many frontiersmen of his day, he held the Indian race in little esteem and, as we shall see, he did not scruple to treat them with the basest kind of treachery. The plea may be made that he was apprehensive of duplicity on the part of the Mohawk chief, but this does not wholly excuse his conduct.

After duly making his plans, Herkimer invited Brant to meet him at Unadilla, on the Susquehanna, higher up than Oquaga. He arrived at this place in the month of July with three hundred and eighty militiamen, but had to wait a week before Brant put in an appearance. The fact that he came with such a numerous escort was well fitted to cause suspicion. Captain Brant also came with a large contingent of warriors, pitched his camp at some little distance from the Americans, and sent a runner to ask the general why he had been honoured with this visit. Herkimer replied that he merely wished to have a talk with his brother Brant and that would be all. The runner said he would bear the message back, but first asked slyly whether all these men were anxious to talk with the War Chief also. Before departing, Brant's messenger signified that the colonials must not trespass upon the field that stretched away towards the Indians' camp. About half-way between the two parties a shed was now put up, large enough to seat two hundred people. It was agreed that each side should send a deputation to this hall, where a meeting would be held. On no account, however, were any firearms or other weapons to be brought from the camps.

Upon the day appointed Herkimer was the first to reach the spot, while Brant arrived a little later. The Indian chief had scented danger and was strictly on his guard. With him were two pale-faces, a Mohawk chief, about two score warriors, and an Indian woman. It was the custom in such a parley to draw a circle on the ground and for the leaders to stand or sit within this. Herkimer and two officers entered the circle, while Brant was accompanied by the inferior chieftain. Brant was all the time watching the general like a hawk and again asked him what was the meaning of his visit. Herkimer repeated that it was only for the sake of good fellowship.

'And all these have come on a friendly visit too?' asked Captain Brant. 'All want to see the poor Indians; it is very kind.' Unaffected by Brant's irony, Herkimer next referred to the troubles between England and the colonies, and tried to draw out Brant. The chief was slow and taciturn in answering, but at last burst forth in no uncertain language. He said that 'the Indians were in concert with the King, as their fathers had been; ... that General Herkimer and his followers had joined the Boston people against their Sovereign.' For all that, he had no fear of the result and knew 'that although the Boston people were resolute, yet the King would humble them.'

The meeting did not break up before there were signs of coming violence, but finally better feelings appeared to prevail and they decided to assemble again on the following morning.

In the interval Herkimer is said to have devised one of the vilest schemes that has ever been charged against a man of his rank. He selected a settler, named Joseph Waggoner, and three other trusty men as his accomplices. These persons were to assist him in a conspiracy against Brant's life that was simply an attempt at murder. The details of the plot were furnished in a confession made afterwards by Waggoner. As the parties stood in the circle, the four accomplices were to take a cue from Herkimer and shoot the Indians down without warning. But Herkimer was reckoning without his host. Joseph Brant was far too shrewd to walk headlong into such an open snare. It is plain that he had come to suspect the intentions of his adversary. Next morning, as he stepped into the circle, he assumed a grave and dignified mien. Addressing Herkimer, he spoke in stern accents:

'I have five hundred warriors with me, armed and ready for battle. You are in my power; but as we have been friends and neighbours, I will not take advantage of you.'

As he ended, a great band of redskins advanced from the engirdling forest, and the war-whoop rent the air. Backed by his faithful warriors, the War Chief could speak in tones of authority to his foe. He did not forget to thank him for his coming, but bade him direct his steps once again towards his home on the Mohawk.

Thereupon Brant turned about and strode away among the trees. Just then thick clouds blotted out the sky; a terrible storm swept in violence across the land, a fitting presage, as men thought, of the scourge of war that must now bring ruin and havoc in its wake.

CHAPTER VII
FORT STANWIX AND ORISKANY

Fresh from undoing Herkimer's ugly plot, Brant abandoned the Susquehanna and went off in the direction of Lake Ontario. A great Indian council was to be held at Oswego, and possibly he was hurrying to this meeting.

A vigorous campaign had been set on foot for the midsummer of 1777 by General Burgoyne, who was now in command of the British forces at Montreal. It was arranged that Burgoyne should strike southward with the main army until he reached the Hudson river. Meanwhile another body of troops, under Lieutenant-Colonel St Leger, would make a long detour by way of Lake Ontario and the western part of the colony of New York. The object of this latter movement was to rally the Indians, collect a force of loyalists, and fight through the heart of the country with the hope of forming a junction with Burgoyne's army at Albany.

St Leger reached Oswego about the middle of July. There he was joined by a regiment of loyalists, the famous Royal Greens, and a company of Tory Rangers under Colonel John Butler. Brant was present with two hundred Mohawks, while a large band of Senecas were also grouped under the king's standard. In all there were seventeen hundred men, fully one thousand of whom were Indians under the supreme command of Captain Brant.

On starting out, St Leger, who knew that a surprise might be attempted, outlined his order of march with great care. A detachment from one of the battalions was sent on ahead, and this was later joined by Captain Brant with a party of his warriors. Five columns of Indians went in front, in single file; the flanks also were protected by Indians at a distance of one hundred paces from the central column.

It was intended that the first blow should be struck at Fort Stanwix, on the head-waters of the Mohawk. This was an old English stronghold that had fallen into decay, but was being repaired and defended in the interest of the revolting colonies by Colonel Peter Gansevoort. It lay on the traffic-road to Oneida Lake, and was considered a strong point of vantage. Its garrison was made up of about seven hundred and fifty colonials. They had provisions enough to last for six weeks and a goodly supply of ammunition, and hoped to be able to withstand attack until help should arrive.

The English leader reached this fort on August 3, and immediately began to invest it. A demand was sent in under a flag of truce calling upon the garrison to surrender. St Leger said it was his desire 'to spare when possible' and only 'to strike where necessary.' He was willing to buy their stock of provisions and grant security to all within the fort. The offer was generous, but the garrison rejected it with a good-tempered disdain and the siege went on with renewed earnestness. The Indians, hiding in the thickets, poured their fire upon those who were working on the walls. The presence of the savages lent a weird fury to the scene, made it, indeed, well-nigh uncanny. One evening in particular they 'spread themselves through the woods, completely encircling the Fort, and commenced a terrible yelling, which was continued at intervals the greater part of the night.' Fort Stanwix was soon in dire straits. The news of the investment had sent a thrill through the whole of the Mohawk valley. The colonials came together in haste, and soon about a thousand of them, led by Nicholas Herkimer, were ascending the river in straggling array. They hurried on their course with such zeal that they did not even send out scouting parties to warn them of danger and prevent surprise. On August 5 this relief force was close to Oriskany, and only eight miles distant from St Leger's position. Herkimer now matured a clever plan, the success of which he confidently expected would bring him victory. He chose three men and sent them forward to gain entrance to the fort and to tell Gansevoort that help was coming. The moment they arrived the besieged were to fire three guns in rapid succession. This was to be Herkimer's signal; he would speed at once along the road to the British position and fling himself on its rear, while, at the same time, Gansevoort must issue forth and attack it in front. St Leger's army, it was hoped, would crumble in hopeless defeat between two shattering fires.

As fortune would have it, this ruse was doomed to complete failure. The messengers set out at eleven o'clock at night, and Herkimer thought they would surely reach the fort by three in the morning. But he waited in vain the whole night through; no sound of cannonade disturbed the quiet air. As the hours crept by his officers became fretful and impatient; in the end they declared for an immediate advance, denouncing Herkimer as a faltering coward. At length the old man, sorely against his will, gave the order to march. The relief party streamed through the forest with disordered ranks. In the meantime Brant's Indians had not been idle. They had carefully watched the manoeuvres of the hostile force, and had given timely warning. St Leger at once took steps to bar the road to attack. For this purpose a division of the Royal Greens was detailed, as well as the Tory Rangers, with Butler in command. The bulk of the contingent, however, were Indians, and it fell to the lot of Joseph Brant to fasten Herkimer in the strong meshes of his net.

The ground over which the Americans had to pass was uneven, and this had not escaped the watchful eye of Brant. He was an adept in the tactics of Indian warfare, and now used his knowledge to good effect. Herkimer had not gone far along the narrow trail before he found himself in difficulties. The road slanted down into a boggy hollow some six or seven miles below Fort Stanwix. This hollow had a winding course in the form of a crescent, and across its march a causeway of heavy logs had been built. Between the ends of the encircling ravine there was an elevated position, thickly wooded and dry. Upon this Brant had laid his ambush, having posted his men with only a slight opening in their ranks towards the incline of the road.

Down into the gully came the colonials, their wagons and a small guard bringing up the rear. As they toiled up the opposing ascent, the gap was closed upon them, and they were surrounded on every side. The rear-guard were left behind with the wagons and fled in a tumult, with a throng of Indians in close pursuit. From the sheltering trees a deadly fusillade swept the hapless files of those who were hemmed about on the rising ground. Darting from their cover, the Indians sprang upon such as lay wounded and dispatched them with knife and tomahawk.

The first onslaught had resulted in a carnival of blood. Now the colonials, owing to their numbers, were able to get together and to place themselves on the defensive. The fight soon became hand to hand and there ensued one of the most gruesome melees of the whole War of the Revolution. The men were able to look into one another's faces; they fought at quarters too close for bullets, and relied upon gun-stock, knife-blade, and bayonet. There was slashing and cutting, clubbing and throttling, and often in their frenzy they grappled tight and died in one another's fast embrace. In the midst of it all Herkimer proved himself no craven. With his leg ripped by a bullet he propped himself against a tree, lit his pipe, and directed the order of the battle. Above the din rang out clear the wild cries of the red men, their painted bodies flashing bright among the trees. In the forefront was Brant, fighting vehemently, his towering form set firmly, his deep voice echoing loud.

While the battle was at its height, rolling clouds had gathered and a drenching storm checked the combatants in their work of slaughter. The colonials were still fighting desperately, but for them the day was lost. After the few moments' interval they re-formed their scattered ranks and resolutely faced the foe. No sooner, however, had the struggle again commenced than the noise of cannon came reverberating upon the moist air. The appointed messengers had arrived at Fort Stanwix, many hours late, and the signal had been given. Deceived by the cannonading and fearing that St Leger might be in distress, the loyalists rapidly drew off with their Indian allies, leaving their opponents on the crimson field. But so exhausted were the colonials by the fierce fighting they had experienced that they could not follow after the retreating army and were forced to move dejectedly down the Mohawk valley. Four hundred of their men had fallen in the battle, dead or wounded, nearly half the number that had entered the swampy ravine. On a litter of green boughs General Herkimer was carried to his stone house on the river, where, a few weeks after the cruel fight, he died with the same fortitude that he had shown when under fire.

The laurels for this victory at Oriskany rested with Captain Brant. He had commanded the greater part of the loyalist forces and his plan had placed the enemy at their mercy. Thanks to this success, the colonials had received a stunning blow, and Colonel St Leger's army was possibly saved from an utter rout. But the Indians had paid a heavy price for their victory; many of their chiefs and warriors lay dead upon the field.

The siege of Fort Stanwix was kept up until August 22. By this time St Leger had reached a point one hundred and fifty yards from its outer wall. During the interval the word of Herkimer's defeat had brought General Arnold with a strong body of militiamen to the rescue. While still some distance away this commander thought that he might create a false alarm in the English camp. A half-witted fellow, who went by the name of Hon-Yost Schuyler, had been captured and was in Arnold's camp. He was freed on condition that he should go to the English camp and give an exaggerated account of the new force which was coming to the relief of Fort Stanwix. When he reached the camp Schuyler went first among the Indians, showing a coat riddled with bullets, and told of the host that was on its way. When asked how many there were, he pointed to the fluttering leaves above his head. The redskins always had a superstitious awe of this stupid fellow and now they were terror-stricken by his words and antics. Panic seized the besiegers. Perhaps Brant tried to quell the disorder, but, if he did, his efforts were in vain. St Leger himself seemed to share in the panic, for he beat a hasty retreat, following the road leading to Oswego. But the War Chief of the Six Nations--it is pleasant to relate--did not retreat with him. While St Leger journeyed to the north, Brant had called together a band of his willing followers. Then he took one of those flying marches which made him famous in border warfare. Crossing the territory of the enemy with great skill and daring, he hurried eastward, and in a short time he was in the camp of General Burgoyne on the banks of the Hudson.

CHAPTER VIII
FIGHTING ON THE FRONTIER

Brant was now regularly in the pay of the British, and until the close of the war he was to be employed actively in weakening the colonists by destroying their settlements intervening between the populous centres of the Atlantic states and the borders of Canada. In this unhappy fratricidal war each side used the Indians to strike terror into the hearts of its enemies, and as a result, in the quiet valleys lying between the Hudson and Ohio and the Great Lakes, there was an appalling destruction of property and loss of life. Brant proved himself one of the most successful of the leaders in this border warfare, and while he does not seem ever to have been guilty of wanton cruelty himself, those under him, on more than one occasion, ruthlessly murdered their foes, irrespective of age or sex. That he tacitly permitted his followers to murder and scalp unarmed settlers shows that he was still much of a savage. As one historian has written: 'He was not a devil, and not an angel.' It is true, as we shall see, that on several occasions he intervened to save Tory friends and acquaintances, but these are isolated examples, and his raids were accompanied by all the horrors of Indian warfare. The only excuse that can be offered for him is that he was no worse than his age, and that the white loyalist leaders, such as the Butlers, as well as the colonial commanders of the revolutionists, were equally callous regarding the destruction of property and life.

Brant appears to have spent the winter of 1777 and 1778 in Canada, but with the opening of military operations in the spring he was again at Oquaga and Unadilla. One of his first exploits of the year 1778 was at Springfield, a small settlement lying some miles beyond Cherry Valley at the head of Lake Otsego. When news of Brant's approach reached this place, a number of the men-folk fled for their lives. Those who remained were taken prisoners. The chief gathered the women and children into one house and set the torch to all the other buildings in the settlement. Brant's care for the weaker sex and the children during this expedition shows that he had a tenderness of heart unusual among the red men of his time.

During the hay-making season the chief was reconnoitring in the Schoharie district, which was situated some distance west of Albany and south of the Mohawk river. The scythe had been at work in the tall grass, and a farmer's lad was busy in a sunlit meadow raking hay. As he dragged the loose bundles over the stubble, he heard a footfall in his rear. Turning about he saw that a sturdy Indian dressed in warrior's garb had stolen upon him. The boy involuntarily raised his rake as though to strike.

'Do not be afraid, young man,' the intruder said in good English; 'I will not hurt you.'

The warrior then asked the youth in friendly terms where a Mr Foster, a loyalist, had his dwelling. He went further and asked the lad his name.

'I know your father well,' said the redskin, when the boy had answered his questions; 'he lives neighbour to Captain McKean. I know McKean very well, and a fine fellow he is too.'

The boy was now quite reassured that the Indian would do him no harm, and boldly inquired who his interrogator might be.

'My name is Brant,' answered the redskin, although he pondered for a moment before replying.

'What! Joseph Brant?' said the youth, as a sharp thrill went coursing through his veins.

'No!' answered the warrior, 'I am a cousin of his'; but a smile lit up his dark countenance, and the boy knew that his denial was just a bit of native humour. Thereupon Brant disappeared in the direction of Foster's house. The boy at once rushed from the field to the fortified post near by to tell his story, and a hue and cry was soon raised. A party hurried to the loyalist's house to seek Brant, but he was not there. Foster said that he had never come and that he knew nothing of him. So, checkmated in their search, the group of would-be captors had to wheel about and go back disappointed to their fortress.

Brant was fast gaining an unsavoury reputation which he but partly merited. Owing to the character of the country in which he was fighting, and to the lack of discipline in the force under his command, destruction of property and plunder were certain to occur. Brant, as we shall see, did little to discourage this among his warriors. His argument was that his antagonists had taken up arms against their lawful king. As rebels, their lands and property were forfeited to the crown and were justly liable to seizure by the king's forces. To the settlers on the border, however, Brant was looked upon as a ruthless marauder, thirsting for blood. Whenever acts of wanton cruelty took place, the blame was generally laid at his door. This explains the bitterness of their attitude to him both during and after the conflict and the singular fear which his name inspired among them.

At Unadilla Brant had begun to fortify an area which lent itself to defence, and thither the tribesmen flocked from the surrounding districts. So determined were the settlers to capture him that they offered a reward to any one who would bring them any knowledge of his movements. Even men like Captain McKean, whom Brant had mentioned so kindly to the farmer's boy, were hot upon his trail. This officer set out with five other men in order, if possible, to effect Brant's capture. While on their quest the little party came one night to the house of a Quaker. To their great delight, the Quaker told them that Brant had been at his place during the day and would come back. He warned them, however, that Brant was prepared to meet them, and that if he returned suddenly their lives would be in danger. McKean, however, was stubborn in his resolve to stay.

'Your house, friend Sleeper,' he said, with a show of bravado, 'shall be my fort to-night.'

But the Quaker would have none of them, and sent the searchers on their way. Then Captain McKean wrote a letter to Brant. Placing this in a stick, he cast it on an Indian path, where it was soon found by a redskin and carried to the War Chief's wigwam. In the letter McKean arraigned Brant for the ferocious manner in which he was fighting, and dared the Mohawk chief to single combat, or to send a chosen body of men to meet him in fair field against an equal number. If he showed his face in Cherry Valley, threatened McKean, 'they would change him from a Brant into a Goose.'

Brant knew the impulsive nature of McKean and took this amusing letter for what it was worth. Yet the letter was not without its effect upon him. They had dared him; they had taunted him with threats; he would show them that Joseph

Brant would have a day of reckoning and that right early. 'Cherry Valley people,' he wrote in the postscript of a short note sent to an ardent loyalist, '[are] very bold, and intended to make nothing of us; they call us wild geese, but I know the contrary.'

Early in July a bloody engagement had occurred in the valley of Wyoming, an extensive region in Pennsylvania on the north branch of the Susquehanna river. For many years after the encounter it was commonly believed that Brant was the leader of the Indians who took part in it. The valley of Wyoming had once been a possession of the tribes of the Six Nations but, in 1754, they had been ousted from their inheritance by a colonizing company. When the Revolutionary War began it was already well peopled with settlers. Naturally eager for vengeance, the dispossessed Indians invited the co-operation of Colonel John Butler and his rangers in a raid. Butler accepted the invitation, and the Indians and rangers to the number of five hundred made a swift descent of the Susquehanna and invaded the valley. Their approach, however, had been discovered, and the entire militia of the district, mustering eight hundred, advanced against them. In the battle which followed, the defenders were defeated with great slaughter and many scalps were taken. Older American historians misrepresented the fight as a cruel massacre of non-combatants and asserted that Brant was present. British writers, following them, fell into the same error. Thomas Campbell's poem, 'Gertrude of Wyoming,' written in 1809, gives a gruesome picture of the episode, telling of the work which was done by the 'monster Brant.' During his visit to England in 1823, the War Chief's youngest son, John Brant, vindicated his father in a letter to Campbell, and showed that the reference to his father in this poem was based on false information. He declared that 'living witnesses' had convinced him that his father was not in the neighbourhood of Wyoming at the time of the so-called massacre; testimony has been forthcoming to support the claims which John Brant then made. It has been shown that the tribesmen of the Six Nations whom Butler had with him were Senecas, while the rest were Indians from the western tribes, and that Brant's tribe, the Mohawks, were not present. Nevertheless the Wyoming slaughter differs only in degree from other scenes of bloodshed and plunder in which Brant took part. In the month, indeed, in which the vale of Wyoming was being bathed in blood, he swept down on the little hamlet of Andrustown, and, bearing away a few captives and much booty, disappeared with his followers in the surrounding forest.

It was now nearing the time of harvest, and in the Mohawk valley the grain had ripened to a golden brown. Even amid the din of war men must live, and so the settlers began to garner the season's crop. Nowhere on the river were there fuller barns than in the populous district that went by the name of the German Flatts. Bordering the Mohawk river on either side, it stretched for ten miles along the valley, rich in soil, and with broad green pastures and plenteous herds. The settlers knew that the enemy was not far off, and they grew more afraid of attack with each passing day. They had two strongholds to which they could flee in case of trouble, Fort Herkimer on one bank of the river, Fort Dayton on the other; but these would be of little use to the settlers if they had not sufficient warning of the approach of the enemy. Mindful of this, they sent four of their number to act as scouts and to warn the settlement of any danger. While on this mission three of the party met with death at the hands of their adversaries, but the fourth escaped and hastened back to the German Flatts. One evening, just before sunset, he arrived with the fearful tidings that Brant was moving up the river with a large band of Indians and would soon be upon them. The alarm was spread through the valley, and men, women, and children gathered up what articles of value they could take with them in their hurried flight, and rushed pell-mell to the forts. During the evening some carried off a portion of their household effects in small boats. In the meantime Caldwell, commanding a party of rangers, with Indians under Brant, had come to the outskirts of the settlement. Then, even before the first gleam of daylight had begun to slant across the valley, the Indians were flitting like ghostly spectres in and out among the buildings. Almost at the same moment flames arose in every direction, flashing and darting against the morning sky. Powerless to stay the destruction, the settlers, huddled behind their defences, witnessed a melancholy sight. Houses and barns, everything that could be given to the fire, were soon a heap of smoking embers.

Caldwell had no means of laying siege to the forts, as he was without cannon; so he made no effort to effect their capture. But he did not check his warriors from roaming at will over the valley. Running down the slopes into the pasture land, they rounded up the horses, the herds of black cattle, and the browsing sheep; and, having collected these together, they drove them from the meadows and disappeared with them among the trees. Before sundown they were many miles away, leaving behind desolation and blank dismay.

CHAPTER IX
CHERRY VALLEY

The next occurrences in Brant's life are even more deplorable than those narrated in the preceding chapter. The Cherry Valley episode can only be regarded as a sad instance of what the use of Indian allies sometimes involved. A peaceful farming district was devastated; peasants were plundered and slain. It is true that some of them were in arms against British rule, but as a whole they were quietly engaged in farming operations, striving to build up homes for themselves on the outskirts of civilization. In this work of devastation and death Brant was only second in command; the leader was a white man and a British officer. But neither Brant nor Butler, who commanded the expedition, was able to restrain the cruelty and ferocity of the Indian warriors until much havoc had been wrought.

A haze was now brooding over the Susquehanna, and the autumn leaves were being tinged with red. The struggle of the year 1778 seemed over and Brant decided to spend the winter at Niagara. Accordingly he set out with a band of warriors from his entrenched position at Unadilla and went forward by easy stages along the old and well-beaten Indian trail leading towards Lake Ontario. He had proceeded well on his way when, to his surprise, a party of former allies crossed his path in the forest. Led by Captain Walter N. Butler, a son of Colonel John Butler, the victorious leader at Wyoming, a body of the Tory Rangers who had been with Brant at Oriskany were going eastward. In 1777 their youthful officer had suffered harsh imprisonment among the enemy, and, burning for vengeance, he was making a late-season tramp into the rebels' country. He had asked for a number of his father's rangers, and his request had been granted. He was also allowed the privilege of taking Brant along with him, should the chieftain be found willing to join his force.

On meeting with Brant so opportunely by the way, he gave him an outline of the measures of retaliation which he proposed to adopt. As the scheme was unfolded, the war-scarred chief of the Mohawks saw that he was meant to serve under this youth of small experience. Brant was ready for almost any work that might be of service to his king, but he was at first reluctant to serve under Butler. The situation between the two leaders became strained, but at last Brant gave in; their differences were patched up, and the two men came to friendly terms. Orders were issued by Brant to his motley throng of redskins, and five hundred of them reversed their march. The united contingent of seven hundred men first headed for the banks of the Tioga river, one of the branches of the Susquehanna. Here a conference was held, and it was agreed that they should make a combined attack upon the settlers of Cherry Valley. To Butler this was more than pleasing, eager as he was to pay off what he considered a heavy score. The heart of the War Chief throbbed with savage delight. A flaunting challenge still rang in his ears; the settlers had invited him to enter their valley, and now he would answer their gibing call. Little did the inhabitants of Cherry Valley dream what was in store for them. During the summer they had carried most of their movable property to a well-built fortress. But as everything had now grown tranquil, they had taken it back to their homes again. Yet hardly had this been accomplished before Colonel Ichabod Alden, commandant of the fort, received a note from an official source telling him that enemies were near at hand.

In spite of the trustworthy source from which it came, Colonel Alden gave barely any heed to this warning message. He declared that the threatened danger was but an idle rumour, that all would be well, and that he would take every precaution for the safety of his people. On November 9 spies were sent out in different directions with a view to getting fuller information. One body of these went boldly down the Susquehanna, where their own carelessness brought about their undoing. At nightfall they lit a fire, and, wrapping themselves up snugly, had gone fast asleep. But to their astonishment, as they rubbed their eyes in the light of morning, they were surrounded by a party of Indians, were bundled off as prisoners of war, and hurried into the presence of Brant and Butler, who extracted much useful information from them. In the light of this information plans were made for an immediate attack on the settlement in Cherry Valley. The settlers were still unsuspecting, when, on the evening of November 10, the enemy arrived within a mile of the fort and crept to the summit of a hill densely shaded by evergreens, and hid themselves from sight. The snow was fluttering down, but towards morning this had changed to a drizzling rain, and the air was thick and murky. Groping their way forward as silently as possible, they stole upon the slumbering cluster of habitations. Just as they came near the edge of the village, a settler was seen riding in on horseback. An Indian fired and wounded him. But the man clung to his horse and pressed on heroically to sound the alarm. Before rushing to the onslaught, the Rangers, under the immediate command of Butler, paused a moment to see what damage their powder had taken through the wet. This moment was fatal for the settlement, for the Indians now rushed on in advance and sped into the doomed village like hounds let slip from their leashes.

The savages were now beyond control, and Brant knew that even he could not stay the slaughter. Fiercest of all were the Senecas, who tomahawked and slew with the relentless fury of demons. But the War Chief thought of the family of a Mr Wells, whom he knew and hoped that he might save. He took a short cut for this settler's house, but the way lay across a ploughed field, and as he ran the earth yielded under his feet and he made slow progress through the heavy soil. When he came to the house, he saw that it was already too late. The Senecas and other Indians with them had done their work. Not one of the inmates had escaped the tomahawk.

While the attack upon the houses was in progress, the Indians made several assaults upon the fort, but to no avail. Their work of destruction, however, went on unchecked among the habitations of the settlers. It was not long before flames were mounting in every quarter. Butler, dismayed to see the Indians so completely beyond control, was forced to hold his regular troops in readiness to oppose a sally from the garrison. Brant meanwhile exerted himself in performing numerous acts of kindness, and did what he could to check the rude violence of his savage band. In one house he found a peasant woman working calmly at her daily toil.

'Are you thus engaged,' he questioned, 'while all your neighbours are murdered around you?'

'We are the king's people,' was the simple response.

'That plea will not avail you to-day,' said the chieftain. 'They have murdered

Mr Wells's family, who were as dear to me as my own.'

'But,' replied the woman, 'there is one Joseph Brant: if he is with the Indians, he will save us.'

'I am Joseph Brant,' came the rapid answer, 'but I have not the command, and I know not that I can save you.'

No sooner had he done speaking than his sharp eye detected a group of Senecas coming to the house. 'Get into bed quick,' he said abruptly, 'and feign yourself sick.' The woman did his bidding, and the Indians when they entered were completely deceived by her pretence. Then, as they departed, Brant gave a piercing signal, and some of his Mohawks gathered into the room. He had called them to help him save this woman and her family. His mark on them would, he believed, make them safe even in this time of general slaughter. He had no colouring matter with him and he asked the Mohawks to use theirs. With deft fingers the Indians then placed the chief's own mark upon the woman and her children in order to protect them.

'You are now probably safe,' said Brant and moved out again into the smoke of fire and battle.

When the massacre was over, it was found that thirty or forty settlers had escaped death and had been made prisoners. From one of these Brant made inquiries respecting the whereabouts of Captain McKean. He learned that this officer had taken his family away to the Mohawk valley.

'He sent me a challenge once,' remarked Brant; 'I have now come to accept it. He is a fine soldier thus to retreat.'

'Captain McKean,' was the rejoinder, 'would not turn his back upon an enemy where there was a possibility of success.'

'I know it,' said Brant, with open generosity. 'He is a brave man, and I would have given more to take him than any other man in Cherry Valley. But,' he added, 'I would not have hurt a hair of his head.'

On the evening of the day of carnage the prisoners were led down the valley to the loyalist encampment, several miles to the south of the fort. Fires had been lighted on every side, and within the extensive range of these fires the luckless captives were corralled for the night. But the air was chill, and many who were clothed in scanty fashion passed the hours of darkness in helpless agony on the cold, bare ground. During the night the shrill cries of the Indians, as they gloated over the scene of their triumph, resounded through the forest. The spoils were divided among the raiders, and with the dawning of another day they set out in the direction of Niagara.

The captives were separated into small parties, and apportioned among the different sections of the force. They had expected little mercy from the victors, but to their surprise clemency was shown to them. Butler had now succeeded in reasserting his authority on their behalf. As the marching bands came to a standstill, they were collected together and the women and children were released. Only the wives of two colonial officers with their families were held captive and carried away into the western forests. In Cherry Valley heaps of smoking debris were all that remained. Groups of redskins still hovered about the unhappy village until, on the following day, they saw that an enemy was approaching. A body of militia had come from the Mohawk river, but they were too late; the savages, avoiding an encounter, departed, and the scene was one of havoc and desolation. As one chronicler has written: 'The cocks crowed from the tops of the forest trees, and the dogs howled through the fields and woods.'

CHAPTER X
MINISINK AND THE CHEMUNG RIVER

Brant now proceeded to the loyalist rendezvous at Niagara, but his restless spirit would not allow him to remain idle. He was soon intent on forwarding a design of far-reaching import, in the prosecution of which he hoped to receive the assistance of the western tribes. He held intercourse with the Delawares and the Shawnees, and planned a joint campaign with them to take place during the winter months. The Western Indians were to make an attack on the borders of Virginia, while he would lead an expedition into the heart of the colony of New York. This bold enterprise, however, was fated to miscarry. Word came that Governor Hamilton, the British commander of Fort Detroit, had been overpowered by Colonel George Clark, in February, on the Wabash river. Hamilton, who had captured Fort Vincennes there, had for some time been endeavouring to interest the western tribes in the British cause; but, on July 5, 1778, Clark had captured the town of Kaskaskia in the Illinois country, and, after a forced march from that place to the Wabash with his Virginia militia, had appeared at Fort Vincennes and compelled Hamilton to surrender. The blow was a severe one and robbed the western tribes of their courage; they were so discomfited, indeed, that they would not venture into the country of the enemy. Balked in his purpose, Brant was forced to remain inactive at headquarters.

During the spring of 1779 the whole struggle in America was rather bare of events. The raids against Wyoming and Cherry Valley had roused the indignation of the Congress of the United States, and it had turned its attention energetically to the Indian races who were opposed to its rule. They must be crushed at all hazards. On February 25 Congress had voted that means should be taken to bring aid to those settlements which had been suffering from the Indians. A campaign of vengeance into the homeland of the Six Nations was to be the crowning effort of the year. This was the plan. A numerically strong force was to operate under the command of General Sullivan. Sullivan was to move up from Pennsylvania, and along the Susquehanna until he reached the Tioga river. At the same time, General James Clinton was to advance from the north, meeting his brother officer by the way. The two divisions should then follow the bed of the Chemung river, and sweep mercilessly upon the villages of the Senecas and Cayugas.

Clinton was at Canajoharie Castle on June 16. With difficulty he crossed the twenty-mile portage to Lake Otsego, and by the end of the month was able to tell General Sullivan that he was ready for the last stage of the journey. Sullivan, on the other hand, was making no attempt to hasten. He moved forward at a leisurely pace, and Clinton grew very impatient at the delay. Even Brant marvelled at Sullivan's inaction. The War Chief knew only too well that when the two rebel forces met the struggle to save the homes of his people would be difficult.

At this juncture the great Mohawk lay with a considerable body of warriors at Grassy Brook. He had learned that Minisink in the Shawangunk Mountains close to the New Jersey line was left unguarded, and decided to fall upon it. Taking sixty redskins and twenty-seven white men apparelled as Indians, he advanced so stealthily that his approach was unnoticed. During the night of July 19 he surprised the town, burnt it to the ground, and carried off prisoners and booty.

Orange county, in which Minisink was situated, was at once in a state of tumult. The local militia flocked together, and were eager to follow hard after their daring foe. Some thought it more prudent to stay at home, but the majority wished immediately to take up the chase. The matter was settled when Major Meeker sprang on his horse, waved his sword, and cried with vehemence: 'Let the brave men follow me, the cowards may stay behind.' With this, the ill-advised settlers picked up the trail of the redskins and started in pursuit. A body of scouts who were slightly in the lead emerged, after various exciting adventures, upon the broad hills that skirt the Delaware river. Below them they could see the Indians twining in and out among the trees. The red men were evidently making for a shallow place where they might ford the stream.

To the colonials this seemed a stroke of good fortune. They would dash down the hill and dispute Brant's passage of the river. Acting on the impulse, they swung confidently along, only to find themselves outgeneralled. No sooner had they sunk from sight in the forest than Brant had artfully changed his march. He slipped through a deep ravine and came out on the enemy's rear. Then he chose his own position for an ambush. The Orange county men, looking high and low for the Indians, at length came to a halt, when to their dismay they found that the enemy were posted in an unlooked-for quarter. There, in concealment behind them, lay Brant's force. The War Chief now issued from among his redskins, and made overtures to the opposing force. He advised them to surrender without offering resistance; if they did so he would see that no harm befell them. Should the battle begin, he added, he might be unable to restrain his followers. The only answer which came was a hurtling bullet that clipped a hole through the covering of his belt. In an instant Brant had faced about and disappeared under cover. Straightway the enemy bore down at break-neck speed upon the tree-sheltered lair of the Indians. In wading through a narrow brook that obstructed their advance, their ranks became disordered, and Brant made effective use of the situation. His voice rose in a war-whoop and his warriors sprang into motion. After delivering one sharp, destructive volley, they seized their tomahawks and surged into the midst of their foe. From an hour before noon until sundown, sheltered by trees and rocks, both sides fought stubbornly. At last the whites gave way, and the battle closed with appalling slaughter. Of the retreating remnant thirty survived, while the bodies of many of their comrades were left upon the field of battle. Of those who sought safety by swimming the Delaware, a number were killed in the water by the Indians, who fired upon them as they struggled towards the opposite bank.

After the fight, as Brant traversed the blood-stained field he bent over the wounded form of Gabriel Wisner, who was a magistrate of Orange county. The fallen man, though suffering excruciating pain, was still able to speak, but the chieftain saw that he was dying. There were wolves in the forest, and these would soon visit the scene of carnage. To bear Wisner from the field would avail nothing. For a moment the War Chief debated what he should do. Then, turning the attention of the wounded man in another direction, he poised his hatchet. In a flash it had smitten the skull of the dying magistrate and his misery was at an end. In this act as in others Brant showed that his contact with civilization had not freed him from the basic instincts of his savage nature. Few white men could have performed such a deed even on the field of battle with so much calmness.

Brant now returned to the border country and, together with Sir John Johnson, drew up a plan of defence. It was resolved that they should fortify a position on the Chemung river, to resist the advance of the Americans into the Indian country. The place selected was not far from the village of Newtown. A breastwork was built, half a mile in length, and this was protected on one side by the river and on the other by two stretches of elevated ground. Upon these ridges battalions were placed. But the defenders were able to muster only a comparatively small force, vastly inferior to the foe in numbers. In all, the garrison consisted of about eight hundred men, two-thirds of whom were Indians.

It was barely four weeks after the battle on the Delaware that Generals Sullivan and Clinton joined forces at Tioga. They had a very powerful army, consisting altogether of some five thousand men, including a strong brigade of experienced riflemen and an artillery corps with a number of heavy guns. They had sent out corps of light infantry in advance and were now moving slowly against the defences occupied by the king's forces.

The War Chief was in charge of the Indians, and despite the strength of the opposing force he had resolved to make a determined stand. As the foe came on, he sent out his men in small parties from the works to annoy them and retard their advance. The Indians attacked the invaders after the manner of bush-fighters, firing and then seeking cover while they reloaded their muskets. The conflict that ensued was desperate beyond description. Every bit of cover--bush, tree, or boulder--held its man. With dogged valour the savages stood their ground, till driven back by the very impetus of the onset. The enemy were massed deep in front and but little impression could be made on their compact ranks. More distressing still, the Americans had brought their heavy artillery into play, and it began to thunder against the defences. On this day Brant was an inspiring figure to his thin line of warriors. His resolute countenance gave them hope; his resonant voice rang out strong and clear amid the clamour and spurred them to resist. Wherever the fight was fiercest he made his way, issuing his orders with care, speaking words of cheer, and, in the face of death, striving to stem the current of certain defeat.

Meanwhile General Sullivan had caught sight of the troops that infested the rising ground. A detachment was immediately told off under Major Poor with orders to storm the slopes and drive the defenders from their position. The War Chief grasped the situation in an instant. In a last attempt to save the day, he rallied his warriors and, with the aid of a battalion of Rangers, threw himself with renewed energy into the struggle. But though Brant hurried from place to place with the utmost energy, it soon became evident that the day was lost. The Americans climbed the ascent and, in the teeth of a brave opposition, turned the loyalists' flank. The troops of the enemy began to fold about the garrison.

'Oonah! Oonah!' The savages' doleful cry of retreat vibrated upon the air. Moving towards the stream, redskins and white men crossed it together in headlong flight. It was an Indian custom to carry the dead from the field of battle, but on this occasion so precipitate was their retreat that eleven corpses were left to lie where they had fallen in the struggle. Sullivan and his army had undisputed possession of the field. To Brant and to the men of the Six Nations this was a day of grief and disaster. The gates of their country were thrown open; their villages were left undefended; there was nothing to prevent the ravager from treading down and plundering the fair land of their fathers, the pride of a noble race, the gift of the centuries. But in the light of their conduct at the affair in Cherry Valley it must be said that their fate was not undeserved.

As General Sullivan advanced, burning and devastating, he came at length into the valley of the Genesee. This he made 'a scene of drear and sickening desolation. The Indians were hunted like wild beasts, till neither house nor fruit-tree, nor field of corn, nor inhabitant, remained in the whole country.' One hundred and twenty-eight houses were razed in the town of Genesee. Sullivan became known to the Indians as the 'Town Destroyer.' 'And to this day,' said Cornplanter, in a speech delivered many years afterwards, 'when the name is heard, our women look behind them and turn pale and our children cling close to the necks of their mothers.'

The War Chief had, indeed, been beaten on the Chemung river. And yet, in the hour of defeat, he had added lustre to his name. In the annals of the forest there are few incidents as glorious as this Spartan-like struggle on the frontiers of the Indian country. Points of similarity can be traced between this battle and another which was waged, in 1813, by the great Shawnee warrior Tecumseh, at Moravian Town, on the Canadian Thames. Like Brant, Tecumseh was allied with a force of white men, and, like the chief of the Mohawks in the struggle on the Chemung, Tecumseh played the leading role in the battle of the Thames. In each engagement the fight was against an army much stronger in numbers; in each the defeat was not without honour to the Indian leader.

CHAPTER XI
OVER THE BORDER

Instead of proceeding to attack the strong loyalist fort at Niagara, General Sullivan re-crossed the Genesee on September 16. Lack of provisions, he asserted, was his reason for turning back. Before this, Brant had frustrated a plot which was afoot among the Indians to desert the British cause. Red jacket, an influential chief of the Senecas and a very persuasive orator, had suggested that the Six Nations should negotiate a permanent peace with the colonists. 'What have the English done for us,' he exclaimed, as he pointed in the direction of the Mohawk valley, 'that we should become homeless and helpless for their sakes?' A considerable following embraced the view of the Seneca chieftain, and it was agreed that a runner should be sent to the camp of General Sullivan to acquaint him with their desire to come to terms. If Sullivan was prepared to negotiate with them, he was to be asked to send his proposals under a flag of truce. These proceedings came to Brant's knowledge and, whether his act may be justified or not, he adopted probably the only means of preventing a wholesale desertion to the enemy. He chose two of his trustiest warriors and gave them instructions to waylay the bearers of the flag of truce from Sullivan's camp. The bearers were killed and the proposals of the American commander fell into Brant's hands, and Red Jacket and his party were left to imagine that Sullivan had not been gracious enough even to send them an answer.

Not long after the rout of the Six Nations on the Chemung river and the destruction of their villages the snow had begun to fall. The winter of 1779-80 was an unusually severe one, and the Indians suffered untold hardships through famine and disease. They were driven to trek in great numbers to the vicinity of the English fort at Niagara. Brant was there at this time, and during his sojourn he saw a wedding performed according to the sacred rites of the Anglican Church. He had lost his first wife, the mother of Isaac and Christiana, and had married her half-sister, Susanna; but she also had died childless, and Brant had taken to his tent the daughter of a Mohawk chief, whom he now decided to wed after the manner of the white people. His third bride, who was about twenty-one years of age at the time of her marriage, is known in history as Catherine Brant. She bore Brant three sons and four daughters, and lived for some years after his death. Her father was the leading sachem of the Tortoise clan and consequently she was able to bestow high rank within the Mohawk nation upon her son, Ahyouwaighs, or John Brant.

The story of Brant's part in the War of the Revolution from this time on can be related very briefly. Before spring he was again on the war-path and helped to destroy the villages of the Oneidas, because of their active sympathy for the rebel cause. In the month of April he closed in upon the settlement of Harpersfield and levelled it to the ground. As he was making his way back from the last adventure, he was seized with fever and forced to move by slow stages. He allowed his warriors to travel only every other day. There is an anecdote telling how he cured himself of his malady in a very Indian-like manner. Taking his position on the side of a hill, a haunt of rattlesnakes, he waited till one should crawl out to bask in the sun. When at length a snake showed itself he seized it and bore it to his camp. This reptile was cooked in a broth, and Brant supped eagerly of the hot decoction. And after partaking of this wonderful remedy, according to the story, he was well again in a very short time.

In August of the same year, 1780, Brant again invaded the Mohawk valley. On this occasion he gained his object by an artful device. He learned that some stores were being borne to Fort Schuyler and pretended that he was going to seize them and attack the fort itself. The local militia marched to the fort's defence and, while they were intent on this, Brant doubled back to the rear. Swooping down upon the white settlement at Canajoharie, he laid everything low and carried away captive many women and children. Later in the season he made a similar descent into the Schoharie-kill, but here there is on record to his credit at least one act of kindness. After the raid, a group of settlers were gathered together, telling of all the mishaps that had occurred to them. One sad-eyed woman told of the loss of her husband and several of her children. She had been bereft even of an infant, which had been torn from its cradle. But that morning, while the officers of the colonial camp were seated at their breakfast, a painted redskin sprang into their midst carrying in his arms a slender child and handed a letter to the officer in command. It was the woman's child that he bore, and the letter was from Joseph Brant.

'Sir,' ran the epistle, 'I send you by one of my runners the child which he will deliver, that you may know that whatever others do, I do not make war upon women and children. I am sorry to say that I have those engaged with me in the service who are more savage than the savages themselves.'

The year 1781 brought the war to its climax. On October 19 Lord Cornwallis, hard pressed at Yorktown by an army of sixteen thousand men under Washington and a powerful French fleet under Admiral de Grasse, was forced to surrender. This was the last important episode before peace was arranged. During the summer the War Chief had still been fighting on the border and harassing the country of those who sympathized with the Americans. In August he was found in the west, having defeated a part of Colonel Clark's forces near the Great Miami river, which empties into Lake Erie.

The treaty of peace between Great Britain and the United States of America was signed in November 1782. Canada, Newfoundland, and what are now the Maritime Provinces of the Dominion remained in the hands of the crown, but the independence of the other English colonies in the New World was recognized. In the whole text of the treaty there was not a word about the Six Nations. But all their lands south of Lake Ontario as far as the banks of the Hudson came into the possession of the United States. For some time it seemed as though the Indians' sacrifices on behalf of His Majesty the King were to be reckoned as nothing, and the tribesmen who had been loyal were very wroth. They had fought valiantly for the crown, and now expected that the king should do something for them in return. All that they had to fall back upon was the promise that their rights would be respected when the conflict ended.

'Now is the time for you to help the King,' General Haldimand had said to the assembled redskins in 1775. 'The war has commenced. Assist the King now, and you will find it to your advantage. Go now and fight for your possessions, and, whatever you lose of your property during the war, the King will make up to you when peace returns.'

Sir Guy Carleton had also assured the Indians that money would be spent to give them the same position after the war that they had occupied before it, and that the government would not be lax in dealing with their needs. In 1779, when General Haldimand was already in command of all the forces in Canada, he had reiterated his promises, and said that he would do his best to fulfil them, 'as soon as that happy time [the restoration of peace] should come.'

When the war was ended most of the Mohawk nation were dwelling on the west bank of the Niagara river. They had pitched their wigwams close to the landing-place, now Lewiston, which was some miles above the fort. Their old territory was situated in the heart of the country of their conquerors and to this they could not return with safety. The Senecas, who lived near by, saw how sad was their plight and offered them land upon which they might reside. The Mohawks appreciated the kindness of this proposal of the warlike nation which had fought by their side in the long struggle, but they could not accept the offer. In the words of Brant himself, they were resolved to 'sink or swim' with the English.

To settle the matter the War Chief journeyed down the St Lawrence to confer with the Canadian leaders. At Quebec he met General Haldimand and was welcomed by this officer with the sincerest friendship and given a chance to discuss the unhappy lot of his homeless people. Haldimand said that he would be quite ready to fulfil the promises that he had made during the war. Brant replied that his tribesmen would like to settle on English ground, and named the region on the Bay of Quinte as a spot suited to their needs. These lands were especially fertile and beautiful, and Haldimand was quite willing that the grant should be made in accordance with their wishes. He said that a tract would soon be purchased and given to the warriors of the Six Nations. Brant must have been well accompanied on his journey to the east, since on his way back twenty Indian families turned aside and pitched their abodes in the territory allotted to them on the Bay of Quinte. They were ruled by an Indian named Captain John, and a thriving Mohawk settlement was thus begun. Brant continued his journey along the south side of Lake Ontario, and came once again to Niagara.

But when the War Chief told the waiting redskins of his negotiations with General Haldimand there was a great outcry of dissatisfaction. The Senecas, who were the chief objectors, stated that they could not allow their kinsmen and old comrades-in-arms to go so far away from them as the Bay of Quinte. The Senecas were still afraid that they might have difficulties with the people of the United States, in whose country they were dwelling. The Mohawks must be near at hand to come to their rescue should the hatchet again be upraised.

Brant felt very keenly for the Senecas, who had done him such yeoman service in the war. They could be cruel in combat, but were very loyal to their friends, and he knew that something must be done for them. Accordingly, he repaired a second time to Quebec and again discussed the situation with General Haldimand. The outcome was that he obtained another grant of land, on the Grand river, which runs with a southerly course into the waters of Lake Erie. A tract six miles wide on each side of this stream, extending from its source to its mouth, was allotted to the Six Nations. This beautiful district, bordering on the shore of Lake Erie, only forty miles from the outer fringe of the Seneca villages, was in a direct line of intercourse between the Six Nations and the many tribes of the west and the upper lakes. Brant obtained the title-deeds to this territory for the Indians in the autumn of 1784, under the seal of royal authority. It was a gift, as indicated by the terms of the award, 'which the Mohawks and others of the Six Nations... with their posterity,' were to enjoy for ever.

Having been provided with a new home, the band of copper-hued patriots now began to cross the Niagara. They were loyalists of another than the white race, and, like the other Loyalists, they had left their Long Houses behind in the hands of the stranger. On their bodies were the marks and scars of many a campaign; their limbs had become suppler with the long march and swarthier in the summer sun; they did not dare to cast a glance back at the fair land that had been the hunting-ground of their fathers. With them were their women, dark-eyed Amazons of the north. Their little ones toddled by their side. The journey was shortly over and they beheld the waters of the Grand river, flowing between their narrow banks. Here, in the flowering glades, they raised their tents and lit anew their council fires. Then they toiled up against the current, searching out the borders of their country; down-stream they shot again, their glad eyes beaming as they saw how wide and goodly was their heritage.

The nation of the Mohawks had come to Canada to stay. Among them settled many from their kindred tribes, red men who would not forsake their Great White

Father the King. By the sheltering boughs of the regal maple, the silver-garbed beech, or the drooping willow they built the rough huts of a forest people. Then they tilled the soil, and learned to love their new abode. Although of a ferocious stock, unrivalled in the arts of savage warfare, the Mohawks and other Indians of the Six Nations in Canada have rarely, if ever, been surpassed by any other red men in the ways of peace.

CHAPTER XII
ENGLAND ONCE MORE

Meanwhile, how was it faring with the tribesmen of the Six Nations who had remained in their former territories east of the Niagara? They were anxious to come to terms with the government of the United States, but not by themselves alone. In any treaty which might be made, they wished the concurrence of the western tribes. The officials of the new republic were, however, opposed to this and treated their desire with scant courtesy. In 1784 a conference was called at Fort Stanwix, but the western tribes were not invited to come. While this was taking place, Red Jacket, the Seneca orator, rose in the company of his fellows and uttered a speech burning with eloquence. His attitude towards the Americans had undergone a change since Brant had undone his treachery before the war had closed. The Six Nations should renew the contest, said Red Jacket. Never should they submit to the yoke of their oppressors. On the other hand, Chief Cornplanter, with sounder judgment, argued for peace. It would surely be an unwise thing for the Indians to enter upon a fresh war single-handed, and without the assistance of their former allies, the English.

At length Cornplanter had his way, and on October 22 a treaty was made with the representatives of the United States. By this treaty the Indians were to give up all the prisoners of war still in their hands. Until this was done, six hostages were to be furnished from among their number. At the same time, the boundaries of the country over which they held sway were defined.

Loud murmurs of complaint arose within the Six Nations on the completion of this pact, and no one was more angry than Joseph Brant himself. He was at Quebec, on the point of leaving for England, but he hurried back on learning the terms of the treaty. He was especially exasperated because Aaron Hill, one of the lesser chiefs of the Mohawks, was to be given up as a hostage. Arriving at Cataraqui, Brant, on November 27, sent a long and stirring letter to Colonel Munroe. In this he showed that his Indians were in no way to blame for the retention of prisoners of war. The fight was over, and the Six Nations wanted harmony restored. With considerable feeling, he referred to the 'customs and manners of the Mohawks.' 'They are always active and true,' he protested; 'no double faces at war or any other business.

The difficulty was quickly righted and the War Chief satisfied, but he saw that all the Indian races were in a precarious position and might, sooner or later, be drawn into hostilities. Meanwhile he was meditating a scheme which might be likened to the bold conception of Pontiac. In vision he saw all the Indian tribes united into one far-reaching confederacy for the assertion of their liberties. Brant was of a singularly ambitious disposition and had no humble idea of his own capacities. He pictured himself as the chosen head of such a vast league of the native races. It was with this in view that at this very time he paid a visit to the western tribes and sought to ascertain their ideas upon the subject. At the close of 1785 Brant was ready to make his second journey across the Atlantic. It was indeed fitting, after his years of active service for the crown, that he should do homage once more at the English court. He desired, also, to plead the cause of his Mohawks, who had lost so much in the struggle. It is even likely that he was pondering over his design of uniting all the tribes and wished to disclose this scheme to the home authorities. A striking sketch of the War Chief's appearance during this period is given by the Baroness Riedesel. This talented lady, who had met the Mohawk chief at Quebec, was the wife of the noted general who led a troop of Hessians in the War of the Revolution.

'I saw at this time,' she writes, 'the famous Indian Chief, Captain Brant. His manners are polished: he expressed himself with fluency, and was much esteemed by General Haldimand.' The strenuous scenes through which Brant had lived, indeed, seem to have left but little impression on his face. 'I dined once with him at the General's,' continued the baroness. 'In his dress he showed off to advantage the half military and half savage costume. His countenance was manly and intelligent, and his disposition very mild.'

On his arrival in London for the second time, Brant received a welcome even exceeding that which was given him on his first visit. He was lauded as king of the red men and lord of the boundless forest. In the houses of the most illustrious people in the realm he was given a place of high honour. One of those who took delight in Brant's company was Lord Percy, heir to the dukedom of Northumberland. Lord Percy had served in America and had been adopted, according to Indian custom, into one of the tribes of the Six Nations, and was called in its language the Evergreen Brake. Charles James Fox, the statesman, was also among the admirers of the War Chief. Fox caused a beautiful silver snuff-box to be sent to Brant, engraved with his initials. The Prince of Wales was attracted by the chieftain and took Brant with him on many of his jaunts about the capital. Brant was amazed at some of the places to which his royal conductor resorted. At the royal palace he was warmly greeted by King George and Queen Charlotte and held in high esteem.

His official visit to their Majesties was marked by a somewhat uncommon incident. As a dutiful subject, it was in keeping with tradition that he should kiss the king's hand, but this he refused to do. The War Chief could not bend, even before the greatest of potentates. Turning to the queen, however, after the fashion of a cavalier, Brant said that he would be only too pleased to kiss her hand. George III did not seem in the least annoyed. He appeared rather to be delighted at this courtesy shown his queen, and so the affair passed happily.

One humorous episode which happened during Brant's stay in London caused quite a sensation. Through the good graces of Earl Moira, he was invited to attend a masquerade ball in Mayfair. It was to be a festive event, and people of distinguished rank were expected to be present. Brant did not go to any pains to deck himself out artfully for the occasion, but was attired only in the costume of his tribe. To change his appearance, he painted a portion of his face, and arrived in this guise at the place of entertainment. As he entered the gay ball-room, his lofty plumage swayed grandly and a glittering tomahawk shone from his girdle. The scene that met his eyes was resplendent with life and beauty. Masked figures were flitting by, clad in every imaginable garb. Here was a sleek-faced friar, rotund and merry; there, a gypsy maid, or mild-eyed shepherdess with her stave. Lonely hermits and whimsical jesters, cackling witches, and members of a pilgrim band--all thronged together with laugh or grimace, adding their own peculiar lustre to the brilliant assembly. By and by a Turk came strolling down the floor; he was a diplomat of high degree, and two nymphs from the paradise of Islam hovered near at hand. Suddenly the Turk caught sight of the painted features of the sturdy redskin. He stopped, and fixed the

Indian with his gaze. Here, he thought, was the chance for a bit of frolic. In a moment he had lost his stately demeanour and lurched jocularly towards the warrior. He reached for the Indian's face, thinking it was screened with parchment. The next instant he had tweaked the nose of the great chief of the Six Nations. Above the confusing medley of sounds burst the wild accents of the blood-freezing warwhoop. On the instant Brant's tomahawk was forth from his girdle, and was whirling about the head of the astonished offender. Never had such a cry been heard within the halls of fashion. Faces turned ashen pale and screams resounded through the spacious mansion. Helter-skelter, in every direction, fled the terrified masqueraders. The Moslem thought that his last hour on earth had come. Then Brant's arm fell; his tense features relaxed, and he had become once more the genial 'Captain of the Mohawks.' According to his own declaration, which may or may not have been exactly true, he only intended a playful contribution to the pleasures of the evening. The Turk was calmed, and the frightened company came slowly streaming back. Everything was explained and Brant became a greater hero than ever before. Yet it is hardly likely that the pompous follower of Islam ever forgot the lively scene which his rashness had produced.

Notwithstanding the gay round of entertainment in which he joined, Brant had been attending to the business matters that had brought him to England. He had sent a letter relative to the affairs of the Six Nations to Lord Sydney, the secretary of state for Colonial Affairs, and he delivered a speech upon the same topic in Sydney's presence. He told him of the losses sustained by the Indians, and hoped that a speedy settlement would be made with them by the British government. 'On my mentioning these matters, since my arrival in England,' wrote Brant, 'I am informed that orders are given that this shall be done; which will give great relief and satisfaction to those faithful Indians, who will have spirit to go on, and their hearts [will] be filled with gratitude for the King, their father's, kindness.'

Just before leaving for America, Brant received a letter from Lord Sydney saying that King George desired that the red men should receive justice. 'His Majesty,' said Sydney, 'in consideration of the zealous and hearty exertions of his Indian allies in the support of his cause, and as a proof of his friendly disposition toward them, has been graciously pleased to consent that the losses already certified by the Superintendent-General shall be made good.'

CHAPTER XIII
STATESMAN OF THE TRIBES

When Brant appeared again in the open councils of his people, he found the red men still in a fretful mood. The Treaty of Fort Stanwix was a source of constant aggravation to them. The white settlers were pressing over their frontiers so boldly that the Indians felt that their lands must sooner or later slip from their grasp. England feared an outbreak of war, and the Indians believed that in such a case she would aid them. A proof of this was the manner in which she was keeping garrisons in the western posts which she had agreed to surrender. It is now conceded that this was done because the United States had failed to live up to its pledges. Be that as it may, Joseph Brant was expected in case of hostilities to organize the strong league of native races that he had planned to form.

In November 1786 a great council of Indian tribes was held at Huron Village, on the Detroit river. This was well attended, and its deliberations were very grave. An address, probably written by Brant, was sent by order of the assembled Indians to the Congress of the United States. Peace was desired, but it would be necessary for the Congressional representatives to treat with the redskins as a whole; difficulties had been engendered because the United States had entered into negotiations with separate tribes--'kindled council-fires wherever it saw fit'--without ever deigning to consult the Indians as a whole; this, affirmed the address, must happen no longer.

During the next few years the War Chief was unsparing in his efforts to come to some solution of the problem which the attitude of the United States had presented. He was quite aware that there was not enough concerted action among the various tribes. In his efforts to unite them he was aided and supported in all that he did by the English officials. But, try as Brant might, it seemed impossible to arrive at that wide union among the tribes at which he was aiming. On every hand were differences of opinion and petty jealousies. In 1789 General St Clair, indeed, was able to make two separate treaties with the Indians, much to the delight of the government at Philadelphia. 'I am persuaded,' St Clair wrote confidently, '[that] their general confederacy is entirely broken. Indeed it would not be very difficult, if circumstances required it, to set them at deadly variance.'

But though unwilling to unite, it was with jealous and angry eyes that they watched the white men cross the Ohio. The year 1790 found the western tribes ablaze with passion and again on the war-path against the United States. The Shawnees, Potawatomis, and Miamis were the leaders of the revolt. An expedition under General Harmar marched against them, but it was defeated with great loss. The Six Nations were the next in arms, and fell without mercy on the settlements by the Alleghany river.

The horizon was now dark and it seemed as though a widespread struggle with the Indians was certain to occur. While the British authorities trusted implicitly in Joseph Brant, the executive of the United States was also trying to win his confidence. Both sides clearly recognized that the future of the red men depended largely on the policy that Brant should adopt. To have two great nations each striving to enlist one's services is a fair indication that the possession of those services will give either nation a distinct advantage. Brant did not lack vanity, and on this occasion he was more than flattered. But, to do justice to Brant, it must be admitted that all the time he had been in favour of peace. He did not wish the tribes to go madly into an unequal contest when there was very slight hope of success, and yet he was strongly of the opinion that his people must not bow too readily to the avarice of the paleface. The Ohio river should be the dividing-line between the Indian territories in the west and those of the republic, and by this they must stand or fall.

The government of the United States at length concluded that neither Brant nor the tribes would listen to its terms and that war was inevitable. It determined to carry the fight vigorously into the very strongholds of the western tribes. General St Clair was chosen for this purpose, and he was given a large force to deal with a certain unrest which had developed in the country of the Miamis. What the War Chief had feared was now about to happen. His hatchet was dull and rusted, and he had grown unused to the strain and hazard of the war-path. But could he hold aloof? The 'Long Knives' were moving against the lodges of his brethren in the west, and so he bent his ear once more to hear the warrior's call.

St Clair set out from Fort Washington in September 1791 and proceeded in the direction of the Miami villages, to the south-west of Lake Erie. As he advanced, he found himself worried by bands of redskins who hung upon his line of march. By November 3, however, he had come within fifteen miles of the Indian villages. When he pitched his camp, his army of militiamen and regulars numbered about fourteen hundred men all told. The Indians were also fairly numerous, and were under the guidance of Little Turtle, a brave chief of the Miamis. Though drawn from various nations, their hearts were knit together by the peril which confronted them. Within their ranks were a hundred and fifty stalwarts of the Mohawk tribe, as well as a number of white men and half-breeds from Canada, who had come to their assistance.

When the fight began the Mohawks were seen to do the bidding of a tall and agile chieftain. Though Little Turtle was the nominal leader, it is conceded that the main antagonist whom St Clair had pitted against him in this engagement was Joseph Brant. Having sent his militiamen on in advance, the American general had bivouacked with the regulars by the side of a small stream, which ran into the Wabash. Just before daybreak on November 4, the raw militiamen found themselves suddenly attacked by a force of redskins. The Americans, who were about a quarter of a mile from the principal camp, turned and fled in confusion. This was what the Indians desired. So hotly did the militiamen retreat towards the camp that St Clair's main force was almost carried off its feet. A rally was made, but the Indians dashed forward with swiftness and daring. Following on the heels of the fleeing militiamen, they were soon at the very edge of the encampment. There they began to pick off the American gunners one by one.

In a short time St Clair's invading army was hemmed in on every side and many of his officers had fallen. Charge after charge was made by his men, but all to no avail. At length he saw that the day was lost and gave orders for retreat, hoping to save what was left of his force. A weak spot was found in the redskins' line, and a remnant of St Clair's proud army went free, scurrying off in wild precipitation to Fort Jefferson, thirty miles away. The ground was thickly strewn with their dead. It has been computed that in this battle eight hundred of St Clair's force were killed or wounded.

This disaster in the country of the Miamis showed the United States how hard it would be to break the spirit of the red men. War having effected nothing, it was again decided to resort to entreaty. A number of chiefs of different tribes were invited to go to Philadelphia, and among them was Captain Brant. 'I can assure you,' wrote the secretary of state in the federal government to Brant on February 2, 1792, 'that the President of the United States will be highly gratified by receiving and conversing with a chief of such eminence as you are, on a subject so interesting and important to the human race.' After some persuasion Brant consented to go and, proceeding on horseback by way of the Mohawk valley, he arrived at the capital city on June 20. There he was gladly welcomed, and every effort was made to win him for the United States. 'I was offered a thousand guineas down,' wrote the War Chief at a later time, 'and to have the half-pay and pension I receive from Great Britain doubled, merely on condition that I would use my endeavours to bring about a peace. But this I rejected.' The American authorities then held out an even more tempting bait. They would give him pre-emption rights over land estimated to be worth twenty thousand pounds and an annual allowance of fifteen hundred dollars. But Brant steadfastly refused, and his reason was very plain. How could he accept such a bribe? 'They might expect me,' he said, 'to act contrary to His Majesty's interest and the honour of our nations.' He did, however, promise that he would urge the Miamis to come to terms with the United States, and that he would go to them for that purpose.

As he was on his way home from Philadelphia he found that a Dutch-American, named Dygert, was pursuing him with the intention of making an attempt upon his life. In New York, while he was talking to several officers at his lodgings in Broadway, he happened to peer out, and saw a man in the street below with his eyes intently fixed on the window of his room.

'There is Dygert now,' he cried.

Colonel Willet, one of the officers, went down and accused the man of basely plotting Brant's assassination.

'Do you know,' said the colonel, 'that if you kill that savage, you will be hanged?'

'Who,' said Dygert in surprise, 'would hang me for killing an Indian?'

You will see,' answered Willet; if you execute your purpose, you may depend upon it that you will be hanged up immediately.'

At this the would-be criminal went off and did not trouble the War Chief any more.

On his safe return to Canada Brant was taken ill and was not able to attend a grand council held in the autumn at Au Glaize, on the Great Miami. When the council met it was agreed that hostilities should be suspended until a fresh council should be held at Miami Rapids.

During the winter of 1792-93 Brant received a visit from Simcoe, lieutenant-governor of Upper Canada, at his home on Grand River. This officer, who had lately been installed at Niagara, carried a letter to the War Chief from his old friend Lord Percy, now the Duke of Northumberland, together with a brace of pistols that the duke had sent to him. Simcoe was on his way to Detroit by sled, and stopped for three days at the Mohawk village. A *feu de joie* was fired in his honour, flags were hoisted, and the Indians made a display of their trophies of war.

Brant and some of the redskins accompanied the lieutenant-governor as far as the Thames river, where was situated the village of the Delawares. Here the War Chief was forced to return. Soon afterwards His Excellency again halted at Grand River on his way back. The Indians entertained him in royal style, performing the calumet dance, the feather dance, and several other dances of their tribe.

In the middle of the summer of 1793 a great assembly of Indians took place at Miami Rapids. Commissioners who were sent to represent the United States were not allowed to approach the place of meeting. Brant made three speeches, urging upon the Indians the advisability of peace. But the red men were still headstrong, and the commissioners had to go away without having reached any understanding with them.

The end of the struggle, however, was coming fast. In 1794 General Wayne marched to the neighbourhood of Fort Miami with a numerous force, defeated the Indians at the Fallen Timbers, and drove them before him in all directions. Crestfallen and heartsore, they saw that the day of the white man had come at last. Brant stood by as their helper to the very end, but it availed them little. The Black Snake, as they called General Wayne, had beaten them, and they knew he would beat them again. The tribesmen who had come from the far west withdrew sullenly across the Mississippi, the other races submitted, and the Treaty of Greenville was signed with General Wayne on August 3, 1795. The ox-cart began to rumble north of the Ohio; the tall forests fell before the settler's axe, and the red man lived and walked no more alone by the 'River Beautiful.'

CHAPTER XIV
THE CHURCH BELL RINGS

Joseph Brant had been a valiant warrior; he had dealt with the affairs of the Six Nations wisely and well. But he had never forgotten that one of the first duties of any ruler is to be, in some sense, a priest unto his people. From a lad, he seems to have been a devoted Christian. The alarms of war had drawn his mind for a period, it is true, to worldly considerations alone, but now that strife had ceased he became once more the friend of the missionary and sought to supply the spiritual needs of the tribes over which his influence was felt.

Like every Indian, the wonderful things which Brant saw all about him in nature held his mind in a spell. To him there was One who had created all things, and who was ever ready and willing to sustain His children. On one occasion in council Brant spoke of the primitive freedom of the Indian people, and then exclaimed: 'This country was given to us by the Great Spirit above; we wish to enjoy it.' He went on to tell how the Indians had tried to get peace, how their efforts had failed, and how their patience was now all gone. Yet there was one covert in which they might find shelter in time of storm. 'We therefore throw ourselves,' was his final utterance, 'under the protection of the Great Spirit above, who, we hope, will order all things for the best.'

While Brant was on his second visit to England, the Society for the Propagation of the Gospel in Foreign Parts asked his help in getting out their printed books for the Indians. He willingly assented, and soon had a new edition of the Prayer and Psalm Book in preparation, He translated also the Gospel of St Mark. The Prayer and Psalm Book and his translation of the Gospel of St Mark were issued as one book. The publication of this volume must have brought a feeling of pride to the breast of the Mohawk chief. The book was a work of art, well printed and with some fine engravings. The frontispiece depicted the inside of a chapel, in which the king and queen were standing with a bishop on each side of them. The monarch and his consort were handing sacred books to the Indians, who were clustered about in an expectant attitude.

A few years later Brant translated into the Mohawk tongue the Liturgy of the Anglican Church as well as a doctrinal primer. Copies of these were sent to Harvard University, and its corporation replied with a cordial vote of thanks to the War Chief for his gift. Brant also planned to write a comprehensive history of the Six Nations, but unfortunately this work seems never to have been commenced.

Hardly had the Mohawks settled at Grand River when they began to feel that they should have a church building in which to worship. Funds were gathered, and as early as 1785 they were laying the foundations of a suitable edifice. This building, which was reared in the depths of the forest about two miles from the centre of what is now the city of Brantford, generally went by the name of 'The Old Mohawk Church.' In 1904, on a petition to the king, it was given the title of 'His Majesty's Chapel of the Mohawks.' Thus was restored the name of the church in which the Indians were wont to worship in the Mohawk valley. With its square tower, quaint slender steeple, and the graves of bygone generations of red men who have worshipped in it gathered about its walls, it is a venerable reminder of the past. The Bible which was first used in 'The Old Mohawk Church' was a gift from Queen Anne to the tribesmen in 1712 and was brought to Grand River from their former home on the Mohawk. The silver communion plate was part of a service which had also been presented to them by the same queen before they came to Canada. It was of burnished silver and bore the Royal Coat of Arms. The remaining pieces of this set were given to the Indians who settled in the Bay of Quinte district. In the year 1786 there was sent to the church a large and melodious bell. This was a presentation from the British government, and on it was stamped the arms of the reigning House of Hanover.

In all the wide region later known as the province of Upper Canada, as yet no other Protestant sanctuary had opened its doors for the use of Christian believers. With the erection of this temple of the Mohawks begins the history of the Protestant churches in one of the fairest sections of the Dominion of Canada. It was a sweet and solemn bell that pealed out its message when service was held on those

Sabbaths in pioneer days. Into the solitudes it rang, wakening the stillness, echoing to hill-top, and throbbing down to distant valley. Up and along the river stole the gladsome strain, the first call to prayer ever heard in this scarcely broken wilderness. From among the trees emerged the exiled people of the Long House. They mingled together; they entered the courts of the Great Spirit, silent and full of awe. There they listened to the Gospel story and burst forth into many happy songs of thanksgiving and of love.

Brant was very desirous of securing a missionary who would suit the tastes of all. He tried to get a resident missionary in the person of his friend Davenport Phelps, but the bishop of Quebec refused Phelps ordination; and it was not until 1822, when the New England Company took over the missionary work on the Mohawk reserve, that the Indians of Grand River had a resident pastor. Brant also had won from General Haldimand a promise that a school should be built for the education of the Indian children, and that a flour-mill should be erected for the grinding of corn.

Brant was deeply interested also in the native amusements of the people of the Long House. He seems to have retained a boyish heart in the later years of his life, and he saw with pleasure the sports and pastimes of the Indian youth. Hour after hour he would sit as an honoured spectator watching them play a hard-fought game of lacrosse that required fleetness of foot and straightness of limb. An eye-witness who sat with Brant at one of these games has told of the excitement which the match aroused. On this occasion a great company of Senecas had come all the way from New York state in order to compete for the mastery with their kinsmen, the Mohawks. The contest lasted for three days before the Senecas finally won the valuable stakes which were offered as the prize.

The field which was cleared for the game was fairly extensive, the goals being placed about five hundred feet apart. The teams had sixty men a side. When any one dropped out from either party another was supposed to take his place, and so the energies of the contestants did not flag. The netted rackets employed in the game of lacrosse were three and a half feet in length, straight at the handle but curved at the other end. The broad portion used for throwing or carrying the ball was formed of thongs of deerskin, interwoven and drawn firm and tight. It was a picturesque sight when the opposing teams were ready to commence play. The animated warriors were nude except for a breech-cloth reaching to the knee. When all was in readiness, an Indian maiden came tripping into the centre of the field. She was prettily attired after the custom of her tribe, wore bracelets of silver and a red tiara decked with eagle feathers. Placing the ball among the players, she hurried from the field of play. Two experts from the rival parties then raised the ball between their rackets and strove to make the first successful throw. The great game had now begun, and each time the ball went through a goal it counted one tally. The score-keepers, who were chosen from the older sachems of the tribes, were invested with peculiar powers. If one team was making far less tallies than its opponent, they could diminish its rival's score (without the players' knowledge, however) in order that the contest might be protracted. Games of this vigorous kind have made the athletes of the Six Nations noted in both Canada and the United States down to the present day.

CHAPTER XV
THE PINE-TREE TOTTERS

It came to pass before long that the Indians wished to dispose of some of the land granted to them on Grand River. The United Empire Loyalists and others, lured by the prospect of cheap land, kept crossing into Canada from the United States; accessions to the population of the Great Lakes region had come by immigration from the British Isles, and the country was making forward strides. Straggling settlers and speculators were often anxious to purchase land in the richer districts when they could get it at a low price. It happened, however, that after the redskins had sold and leased bits of their territory to such persons, the provincial government began to interfere. The land, it said, belonged to the Indians only so long as they remained upon it. They could not, therefore, sell any of it, as they had no direct ownership of the soil.

This decision shed a new light upon the proprietary rights of the Six Nations in Canada and the Indians were sorely perplexed. All along they thought that they held their lands like other settlers who had proved their loyalty. Brant vigorously took up their case, made several able speeches on their behalf, and freely corresponded with the authorities of the province regarding the matter. In 1793 Governor Simcoe issued a new proclamation respecting the grant, but this did not end the dispute. The province still claimed the right of pre-emption with respect to the whole of their reserve. Later on the matter was carried to England, and the British government tended to favour the Indians' claims. But nothing was done, owing to contentions among the redskins themselves. It was only, indeed, after Brant's death that the affair was finally settled. The sale of large tracts of Indian land was then authorized, and the money received was safely invested for the benefit of the Mohawks and others of the Six Nations in Canada. In connection with this difficult question Brant had intended making a trip to England, but was forced to abandon the idea.

During the latter part of his life Brant visited different parts of America and twice journeyed as far as the Atlantic seaboard. On these occasions he had the opportunity of talking over old campaigns with officers who had fought against him in the war, and he delighted his listeners with stirring stories of his experiences in the field. On one occasion, when in Philadelphia, he was entertained in sumptuous fashion by Colonel Aaron Burr. A dinner party was held in his honour, and among the guests were Talleyrand and Volney. Early in the evening the War Chief was rather taciturn, and the other guests were somewhat disappointed. But this was only a passing mood, from which Brant soon freed himself. Launching into the conversation, he was soon the centre of attraction.

Though Captain Brant was able to pass his later years in comparative ease, his life was marred by the occurrence of two untoward events. His eldest son, Isaac, was a reprobate over whom the father exercised little influence. Isaac had been guilty of acts of violence and had begun to threaten Joseph Brant himself. He was jealous of the numerous children of Catherine Brant and took occasion to offer her various insults. In 1795 both father and son were at Burlington Heights, at a time when the Indians were receiving supplies from the provincial government. Isaac, crazed with liquor, tried to assault his father in one of the lower rooms of an inn, but he was held in check by several of his youthful companions.

Captain Brant drew a dirk which he usually carried with him, and in the excitement of the moment inflicted a slight wound on Isaac's hand. The cut was not serious, but Isaac would not allow it to be properly treated, and subsequently died from an attack of brain fever. The War Chief was sorely grieved at the result of his hasty action, and fretted about it until the end of his days. He is said to have hung the dirk up in his room and to have often wept as he gazed upon it. The other source of trouble to Brant was the revolt against his rule of a small minority among the tribes. This movement was led by Brant's old adversary, Red Jacket, and another chief, the Farmer's Brother. A council was held by the dissenters at Buffalo Creek in 1803, and Joseph Brant was formally deposed as head of the confederacy of the Six Nations. But as this meeting had not been legally convoked, its decisions were of no validity among the Nations. The following year, at another council, legitimately assembled, the tribesmen openly declared their confidence in the War Chief's rule.

Because of Brant's many services to the crown, the British government gave him a fine stretch of land on the north-west shore of Lake Ontario, near the entrance to Burlington Bay. On his estate, known as Wellington Square, he erected a large two-storey house, in which he might spend the remaining years of his life. A number of black slaves whom he had captured in the war were his servants and gave him every attention. Brant is said to have subjected these negroes to a rigid discipline and to have been more or less of a taskmaster in his treatment of them. In his declining years he was wont to gaze over the waters of Lake Ontario, remembering the country stretching from the southern shore where once he had struggled, and the valley of the Mohawk, where had been the lodges of his people.

But the giant pine-tree of the forest was now beginning to bend. Tall and erect, it had out-topped and outrivalled every other tree of the woodland. Men knew that that pine-tree was tottering. In the autumn of 1807 the Captain of the Six Nations was in the grip of a serious illness. Friends and neighbours came to bring solace and comfort, for he was widely revered. Racked with pain, but uncomplaining, he passed the few weary hours of life which were left. On November 24, 1807, the long trail came to an end. Close by Brant's bedside. John Norton,[9] a chieftain of his tribe, leaned to catch the last faltering word.

'Have pity on the poor Indians,' whispered the dying War Chief; 'if you can get any influence with the great, endeavour to do them all the good you can.'

The body of Captain Brant was taken to Grand River and buried beside the walls of the church he had helped to rear. In the centre of the busy city of Brantford--whose name, as well as that of the county, commemorates his --stands a beautiful monument, picturesque and massive, to his worth and valour; in the hearts of the people of Canada he is enshrined as a loyal subject, a man of noble action, and a dauntless hero. Seldom in the annals of Canada do we find a character so many-sided as the Captain of the Mohawks. He was a child of nature, and she endowed him with many gifts--a stout and hardy frame, a deportment pleasing and attractive, and an eloquent tongue. It was these natural endowments that gave him endurance in the conflict, pre-eminence in council, and that won for him the admiration of his contemporaries.

---

9   Norton was a Scotsman who, coming to Canada early in life, settled among the Mohawks and won a chief's rank among them. He played an important part in the War of 1812.

The education which Brant received was meagre, but he could hardly have put what knowledge he had to better advantage. After he had been relieved from the arduous life of the camp, he began to satisfy again his desires for self-culture. His correspondence towards the close of his life shows a marked improvement in style over that of his earlier years. There is no lack of convincing evidence that Brant had a penetrating and well-balanced intellect; but his chief glory is the constant efforts he put forth for the moral and religious uplift of his people.

With respect to Brant's abilities as a military leader, there will continue to exist differences of opinion. That he possessed the craftiness of his race in a superlative degree, and that he used this to baffle his opponents on the field of battle, cannot be denied. Some will go further and assert that he had a remarkable genius in the art of stratagem. Whatever powers he had he used, from his boyhood days, in the interests of British rule in America, and the services rendered by this last great leader of the Six Nations in the War of the Revolution were not among the least of the influences that enabled Great Britain to maintain a foothold on the North American continent. Joseph Brant in the War of the Revolution and his descendants in the War of 1812 played essential parts in firmly basing British institutions and British rule in Canada.

www.bookjungle.com *email: sales@bookjungle.com fax:* 630-214-0564 *mail:* Book Jungle PO Box 2226 Champaign, IL 61825

The Codes Of Hammurabi And Moses
W. W. Davies

QTY

The discovery of the Hammurabi Code is one of the greatest achievements of archaeology, and is of paramount interest, not only to the student of the Bible, but also to all those interested in ancient history...

Religion ISBN: *1-59462-338-4* Pages:132 *MSRP $12.95*

The Theory of Moral Sentiments
Adam Smith

QTY

This work from 1749. contains original theories of conscience amd moral judgment and it is the foundation for systemof morals.

Philosophy ISBN: *1-59462-777-0* Pages:536 *MSRP $19.95*

Jessica's First Prayer
Hesba Stretton

QTY

In a screened and secluded corner of one of the many railway-bridges which span the streets of London there could be seen a few years ago, from five o'clock every morning until half past eight, a tidily set-out coffee-stall, consisting of a trestle and board, upon which stood two large tin cans, with a small fire of charcoal burning under each so as to keep the coffee boiling during the early hours of the morning when the work-people were thronging into the city on their way to their daily toil...

Childrens ISBN: *1-59462-373-2* Pages:84 *MSRP $9.95*

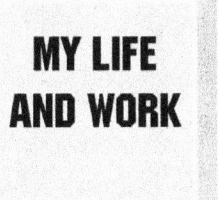

My Life and Work
Henry Ford

QTY

Henry Ford revolutionized the world with his implementation of mass production for the Model T automobile. Gain valuable business insight into his life and work with his own auto-biography... "We have only started on our development of our country we have not as yet, with all our talk of wonderful progress, done more than scratch the surface. The progress has been wonderful enough but..."

Biographies/ ISBN: *1-59462-198-5* Pages:300 *MSRP $21.95*

www.bookjungle.com *email: sales@bookjungle.com fax: 630-214-0564 mail: Book Jungle PO Box 2226 Champaign, IL 61825*

The Art of Cross-Examination
Francis Wellman

QTY

I presume it is the experience of every author, after his first book is published upon an important subject, to be almost overwhelmed with a wealth of ideas and illustrations which could readily have been included in his book, and which to his own mind, at least, seem to make a second edition inevitable. Such certainly was the case with me; and when the first edition had reached its sixth impression in five months, I rejoiced to learn that it seemed to my publishers that the book had met with a sufficiently favorable reception to justify a second and considerably enlarged edition. ..

Reference   ISBN: *1-59462-647-2*   Pages:412   MSRP *$19.95*

On the Duty of Civil Disobedience
Henry David Thoreau

QTY

Thoreau wrote his famous essay, On the Duty of Civil Disobedience, as a protest against an unjust but popular war and the immoral but popular institution of slave-owning. He did more than write—he declined to pay his taxes, and was hauled off to gaol in consequence. Who can say how much this refusal of his hastened the end of the war and of slavery ?

Law   ISBN: *1-59462-747-9*   Pages:48   MSRP *$7.45*

Dream Psychology Psychoanalysis for Beginners
Sigmund Freud

QTY

Sigmund Freud, born Sigismund Schlomo Freud (May 6, 1856 - September 23, 1939), was a Jewish-Austrian neurologist and psychiatrist who co-founded the psychoanalytic school of psychology. Freud is best known for his theories of the unconscious mind, especially involving the mechanism of repression; his redefinition of sexual desire as mobile and directed towards a wide variety of objects; and his therapeutic techniques, especially his understanding of transference in the therapeutic relationship and the presumed value of dreams as sources of insight into unconscious desires.

Psychology   ISBN: *1-59462-905-6*   Pages:196   MSRP *$15.45*

The Miracle of Right Thought
Orison Swett Marden

QTY

Believe with all of your heart that you will do what you were made to do. When the mind has once formed the habit of holding cheerful, happy, prosperous pictures, it will not be easy to form the opposite habit. It does not matter how improbable or how far away this realization may see, or how dark the prospects may be, if we visualize them as best we can, as vividly as possible, hold tenaciously to them and vigorously struggle to attain them, they will gradually become actualized, realized in the life. But a desire, a longing without endeavor, a yearning abandoned or held indifferently will vanish without realization.

Self Help   ISBN: *1-59462-644-8*   Pages:360   MSRP *$25.45* www.bookjungle.com email: sales@bookjungle.com fax: 630-214-0564 mail: Book Jungle PO Box 2226 Champaign, IL 61825

QTY

	Title	ISBN	Price
☐	**The Rosicrucian Cosmo-Conception Mystic Christianity** *by Max Heindel*	ISBN: 1-59462-188-8	$38.95
	The Rosicrucian Cosmo-conception is not dogmatic, neither does it appeal to any other authority than the reason of the student. It is: not controversial, but is: sent forth in the, hope that it may help to clear...	New Age/Religion Pages 646	
☐	**Abandonment To Divine Providence** *by Jean-Pierre de Caussade*	ISBN: 1-59462-228-0	$25.95
	"The Rev. Jean Pierre de Caussade was one of the most remarkable spiritual writers of the Society of Jesus in France in the 18th Century. His death took place at Toulouse in 1751. His works have gone through many editions and have been republished...	Inspirational/Religion Pages 400	
☐	**Mental Chemistry** *by Charles Haanel*	ISBN: 1-59462-192-6	$23.95
	Mental Chemistry allows the change of material conditions by combining and appropriately utilizing the power of the mind. Much like applied chemistry creates something new and unique out of careful combinations of chemicals the mastery of mental chemistry...	New Age Pages 354	
☐	**The Letters of Robert Browning and Elizabeth Barret Barrett 1845-1846 vol II** *by Robert Browning and Elizabeth Barrett*	ISBN: 1-59462-193-4	$35.95
		Biographies Pages 596	
☐	**Gleanings In Genesis (volume I)** *by Arthur W. Pink*	ISBN: 1-59462-130-6	$27.45
	Appropriately has Genesis been termed "the seed plot of the Bible" for in it we have, in germ form, almost all of the great doctrines which are afterwards fully developed in the books of Scripture which follow...	Religion/Inspirational Pages 420	
☐	**The Master Key** *by L. W. de Laurence*	ISBN: 1-59462-001-6	$30.95
	In no branch of human knowledge has there been a more lively increase of the spirit of research during the past few years than in the study of Psychology, Concentration and Mental Discipline. The requests for authentic lessons in Thought Control, Mental Discipline and...	New Age/Business Pages 422	
☐	**The Lesser Key Of Solomon Goetia** *by L. W. de Laurence*	ISBN: 1-59462-092-X	$9.95
	This translation of the first book of the "Lernegton" which is now for the first time made accessible to students of Talismanic Magic was done, after careful collation and edition, from numerous Ancient Manuscripts in Hebrew, Latin, and French...	New Age/Occult Pages 92	
☐	**Rubaiyat Of Omar Khayyam** *by Edward Fitzgerald*	ISBN: 1-59462-332-5	$13.95
	Edward Fitzgerald, whom the world has already learned, in spite of his own efforts to remain within the shadow of anonymity, to look upon as one of the rarest poets of the century, was born at Bredfield, in Suffolk, on the 31st of March, 1809. He was the third son of John Purcell...	Music Pages 172	
☐	**Ancient Law** *by Henry Maine*	ISBN: 1-59462-128-4	$29.95
	The chief object of the following pages is to indicate some of the earliest ideas of mankind, as they are reflected in Ancient Law, and to point out the relation of those ideas to modern thought.	Religiom/History Pages 452	
☐	**Far-Away Stories** *by William J. Locke*	ISBN: 1-59462-129-2	$19.45
	"Good wine needs no bush, but a collection of mixed vintages does. And this book is just such a collection. Some of the stories I do not want to remain buried for ever in the museum files of dead magazine-numbers an author's not unpardonable vanity..."	Fiction Pages 272	
☐	**Life of David Crockett** *by David Crockett*	ISBN: 1-59462-250-7	$27.45
	"Colonel David Crockett was one of the most remarkable men of the times in which he lived. Born in humble life, but gifted with a strong will, an indomitable courage, and unremitting perseverance...	Biographies/New Age Pages 424	
☐	**Lip-Reading** *by Edward Nitchie*	ISBN: 1-59462-206-X	$25.95
	Edward B. Nitchie, founder of the New York School for the Hard of Hearing, now the Nitchie School of Lip-Reading, Inc, wrote "LIP-READING Principles and Practice". The development and perfecting of this meritorious work on lip-reading was an undertaking...	How-to Pages 400	
☐	**A Handbook of Suggestive Therapeutics, Applied Hypnotism, Psychic Science** *by Henry Munro*	ISBN: 1-59462-214-0	$24.95
		Health/New Age/Health/Self-help Pages 376	
☐	**A Doll's House: and Two Other Plays** *by Henrik Ibsen*	ISBN: 1-59462-112-8	$19.95
	Henrik Ibsen created this classic when in revolutionary 1848 Rome. Introducing some striking concepts in playwriting for the realist genre, this play has been studied the world over.	Fiction/Classics/Plays 308	
☐	**The Light of Asia** *by sir Edwin Arnold*	ISBN: 1-59462-204-3	$13.95
	In this poetic masterpiece, Edwin Arnold describes the life and teachings of Buddha. The man who was to become known as Buddha to the world was born as Prince Gautama of India but he rejected the worldly riches and abandoned the reigns of power when...	Religion/History/Biographies Pages 170	
☐	**The Complete Works of Guy de Maupassant** *by Guy de Maupassant*	ISBN: 1-59462-157-8	$16.95
	"For days and days, nights and nights, I had dreamed of that first kiss which was to consecrate our engagement, and I knew not on what spot I should put my lips..."	Fiction/Classics Pages 240	
☐	**The Art of Cross-Examination** *by Francis L. Wellman*	ISBN: 1-59462-309-0	$26.95
	Written by a renowned trial lawyer, Wellman imparts his experience and uses case studies to explain how to use psychology to extract desired information through questioning.	How-to/Science/Reference Pages 408	
☐	**Answered or Unanswered?** *by Louisa Vaughan*	ISBN: 1-59462-248-5	$10.95
	Miracles of Faith in China	Religion Pages 112	
☐	**The Edinburgh Lectures on Mental Science (1909)** *by Thomas*	ISBN: 1-59462-008-3	$11.95
	This book contains the substance of a course of lectures recently given by the writer in the Queen Street Hall, Edinburgh. Its purpose is to indicate the Natural Principles governing the relation between Mental Action and Material Conditions...	New Age/Psychology Pages 148	
☐	**Ayesha** *by H. Rider Haggard*	ISBN: 1-59462-301-5	$24.95
	Verily and indeed it is the unexpected that happens! Probably if there was one person upon the earth from whom the Editor of this, and of a certain previous history, did not expect to hear again...	Classics Pages 380	
☐	**Ayala's Angel** *by Anthony Trollope*	ISBN: 1-59462-352-X	$29.95
	The two girls were both pretty, but Lucy who was twenty-one who supposed to be simple and comparatively unattractive, whereas Ayala was credited, as her Bombwhat romantic name might show, with poetic charm and a taste for romance. Ayala when her father died was nineteen...	Fiction Pages 484	
☐	**The American Commonwealth** *by James Bryce*	ISBN: 1-59462-286-8	$34.45
	An interpretation of American democratic political theory. It examines political mechanics and society from the perspective of Scotsman James Bryce	Politics Pages 572	
☐	**Stories of the Pilgrims** *by Margaret P. Pumphrey*	ISBN: 1-59462-116-0	$17.95
	This book explores pilgrims religious oppression in England as well as their escape to Holland and eventual crossing to America on the Mayflower, and their early days in New England...	History Pages 268	

www.bookjungle.com email: sales@bookjungle.com fax: 630-214-0564 mail: Book Jungle PO Box 2226 Champaign, IL 61825

			QTY
The Fasting Cure *by Sinclair Upton*	ISBN: *1-59462-222-1*	**$13.95**	

In the Cosmopolitan Magazine for May, 1910, and in the Contemporary Review (London) for April, 1910, I published an article dealing with my experiences in fasting. I have written a great many magazine articles, but never one which attracted so much attention... *New Age/Self Help/Health Pages 164*

Hebrew Astrology *by Sepharial* ISBN: *1-59462-308-2* **$13.45**

In these days of advanced thinking it is a matter of common observation that we have left many of the old landmarks behind and that we are now pressing forward to greater heights and to a wider horizon than that which represented the mind-content of our progenitors... *Astrology Pages 144*

Thought Vibration or The Law of Attraction in the Thought World ISBN: *1-59462-127-6* **$12.95**
by William Walker Atkinson *Psychology/Religion Pages 144*

Optimism *by Helen Keller* ISBN: *1-59462-108-X* **$15.95**

Helen Keller was blind, deaf, and mute since 19 months old, yet famously learned how to overcome these handicaps, communicate with the world, and spread her lectures promoting optimism. An inspiring read for everyone... *Biographies/Inspirational Pages 84*

Sara Crewe *by Frances Burnett* ISBN: *1-59462-360-0* **$9.45**

In the first place, Miss Minchin lived in London. Her home was a large, dull, tall one, in a large, dull square, where all the houses were alike, and all the sparrows were alike, and where all the door-knockers made the same heavy sound... *Childrens/Classic Pages 88*

The Autobiography of Benjamin Franklin *by Benjamin Franklin* ISBN: *1-59462-135-7* **$24.95**

The Autobiography of Benjamin Franklin has probably been more extensively read than any other American historical work, and no other book of its kind has had such ups and downs of fortune. Franklin lived for many years in England, where he was agent... *Biographies/History Pages 332*

Name	
Email	
Telephone	
Address	
City, State ZIP	

☐ Credit Card   ☐ Check / Money Order

Credit Card Number	
Expiration Date	
Signature	

Please Mail to: Book Jungle
                    PO Box 2226
                    Champaign, IL 61825
or Fax to: 630-214-0564

ORDERING INFORMATION

web: *www.bookjungle.com*
email: *sales@bookjungle.com*
fax: *630-214-0564*
mail: *Book Jungle PO Box 2226 Champaign, IL 61825*
or PayPal *to sales@bookjungle.com*

Please contact us for bulk discounts

DIRECT-ORDER TERMS

20% Discount if You Order Two or More Books
Free Domestic Shipping!
Accepted: Master Card, Visa, Discover, American Express

www.ingramcontent.com/pod-product-compliance
Lightning Source LLC
Chambersburg PA
CBHW081326040426
42453CB00013B/2313